Elijah Men Eat Meat

© JD Jones 2017

First Edition
ISBN-13: 978-1537764313
ISBN-10: 1537764314

Cover by Stephen Melniszyn of Stephen Melniszyn Designs.

Elijah Men
Eat Meat

Readings to slaughter your inner Ahab & pursue Revival and Reform

The Elijah Readings

Thoughts from British Leaders

Piercing, singeing truth written with Fathering love, which both pulls down and builds up. Joshua serves up a meat feast on the life of the great prophet Elijah that is both a prophetic picture of where we are today in the church calendar and a sobering, thrilling reminder of the great men and women of God who have gone on before us. This book is essential reading for anyone who is serious about putting on some spiritual muscle, isn't afraid of confronting our culture's sacred cows and who wants to walk worthy of the high call in Christ Jesus. Chew and savour slowly.
-**Dominic Muir**, Author of *God Hunger*
Founder of David's Tent and NowBeleive.Com

For all that is unconventional about the style and presentation of this book, the Pastor of Therfield Chapel in Hertfordshire, England has delivered a book to challenge all who name the name of Jesus Christ. Joshua writes with refreshing and unstuffy directness about Elijah's conflict with Ahab, king of Israel, applying numerous spiritual lessons to the compromised and cowardly Church of the 21st century. While the author's style is highly idiosyncratic, his commitment to biblical truth is reassuring in the face of today's apostate liberalism. One may say Joshua reflects something of the fame of Martin Luther (whom he obviously admires) as a popular prophet. I personally find the book irresistibly enlightening. I have no doubt others will find the same. Buy it in quantity and give them away!
-**Dr Alan C. Clifford**, Pastor
Norwich Reformed Church

I highly recommend *Elijah Men* as a powerful book to keep us sharp and shake the slack out of us. It is mature meat for an Elijah generation packaged in small, short chapters. Great for up and coming preachers or any disciple of Christ.
-**Pastor Colin Houston**, Belfast
Director of Trumpeters Voice Foundation

This isn't mere meat. It is rich steak. Don't just read it. Chew it slowly. This is not a book for the faint-hearted. But if you are weak, it will infuse you with courage and strength. Like the biblical prophets, Jones penetrating exegesis, powerful language and robust application dismantles politically correct orthodoxies and empowers his readers with an alternative vision of reality. Honestly, it has been a long time since I read such a firecracker of a book.

-Rev Dr Jules Gomes,
Faculty member for the Oxford Centre for Religion and Public Life

Joshua Jones writes with the same spirit as some of the great prophetic voices of the last century: David Wilkerson, Leonard Ravenhill, Keith Green etc. Yet the subjects he speaks into are timely for the Church of this century. That is because he taps into ancient truths that are applicable for every generation. This book is a challenge and a clarion call for the Church to rediscover what it means to live in the fear of the Lord. It shines a light on important cultural issues bringing both the tears of repentance and the hope that comes from knowing that the God of Elijah is still raising up his champions of truth today."

-Evangelist Andrew Murray,
www.generationbuilders.org

Dedication & Thanks

to my sons Ransom and Elijah, to my godson Malachi Lowe,
and to a generation of young men ravenous for more from God

I'm nowhere near being an Elijah Man.
I'm far too much like Ahab.
And I want my inner Ahab to die.

I am indebted to the 19th Century Methodist minister EM Bounds. His classic, *Power in Prayer* has impacted my life and he his quoted throughout this book. Discerning readers may also hear echoes (albeit feeble and immature echoes) of Andrew Murray, Leonard Ravenhill, AW Pink, and other masters of the prayer closet within these pages.

Thanks my friend Imogen Lowe for her work in proofreading, to Stephen Melniszyn for his cover design, and to my wife for supporting me in taking the time to write all.

Readers, one goal of this project is to unite like-minded hearts. If you are given to social media, please use the hashtag #ElijahMen when sharing anything from the book or even stories of reform revival in your area. Prophetic voices can often be lonely voices and we need the encouragement.

Hello

Martin Luther ignited a world-changing reformation on a door in Wittenberg, Germany on the 31st October 1517. Armed with nothing but words and a hammer, he *protested* against a spiritually bankrupt world and a corrupt priestcraft. He *protested* against religious abuse and the absence of God's word in the language of his people. Thus, *Protestantism* was born.

But this birthday is a dark one for the UK church. Aggressive demands are being made by this generation's zeitgeist on the church and fires of holy resistance are tragically few and far between. A blitzkrieg of LGBT activism has battered us in efforts to squash all dissent to a new view of sexuality and marriage. Qur'anic passages that deny Christ's divinity are now read in our nation's cathedrals at the invitation of ministers. One man who held 'traditional views' on gender was bullied out of becoming a bishop in our midlands. Sadly, many churches have responded with all the fight of a wet croissant. Instead of *protesting* sin, some of us now boast of *affirming* it.

The churches in America and other Western countries also have challenges, but statistically, the church here in Britain is very ill. 71% of those 18-25 now register as 'non-religious'. Faith is alive in some immigrant communities, but among the ethnically British, churches are in sharp decline. One report attests that for every one child from a secular home that finds faith in Christ, twenty-six from Christian homes fall away. In spite of the millions we spend on savvy media and large events, Babylon still devours our children like popcorn—and there is little fervor or faith in the hearts of those who survive to adulthood.

Other surveys indicate that the average Christian now spends 30 minutes *a week* in prayer and 50 minutes *a day* on social media. We are obese physically and skeletally thin spiritually. Our youth do not yearn for the glory of God because they have never seen it all while we hibernate from Biblical truths that once kept our spiritual forbearers ablaze.

It was to a similar comatose generation that Elijah appeared as a rough and roaring alarm clock to rouse the nation he loved. On the 500th birthday of the Reformation, may we also awaken to our impoverishment. Let us pray that God would raise up men to protest sin and light the fires of revival and reform.

It is to that end that I offer up this book. As ravens carried meat to Elijah in the desert, may this book carry nourishment to ravenous souls in dry places.

-Joshua D. Jones
2017, Cambridge

Elijah is coming and will restore everything.

-Jesus

#ElijahMen

Dead

853 B.C.

He listens and sighs. He's just heard the news that's provoking panic all over the nation: *A random arrow has killed the King.*

Our preacher steps aside from his eager apprentice and stands for a moment in the one place where he is always at home: the place of prayer. Since his call to the ministry, his whole life has been consumed with turning the heart of Israel's King back to the God of his fathers.

The preacher already knows how it ended for him. He does not need to be told the particulars. He explained to the monarch this was going to happen years before. He seemed to listen a little at the time. But his behaviour in the years following showed that his heart was still deaf to God. The preacher was hoping he might change. God is merciful after all. And the King did show signs of repentance once—even if they were only small ones. Through countless hours of private prayer, our preacher had come to love this wayward ruler—wicked though he was. *What will his son bring to the nation as the new King?* He already knows. The preacher is aware the throne's successor has a heart set on evil. He is his mother's son.

Our preacher has only been close to two people since he began shouldering this ministry. The first is this young man, his spiritual son and protégé—the guy he couldn't get rid of if he tried. He will take over leadership of the school one day. And the other? A spiritual daughter he acquired during his time in exile. The young widow and her boy.

Our preacher sheds a tear for the tragedy that is Ahab as he buries a spiritual hope. It could have been different. He reflects on the past and trusts God for the future. He looks up at Eternity's throne and whispers a prayer for the nation as it enters a new chapter of history.

How had Ahab gotten here? How had he?

Profile: Ahab

'Ahab did more of what Yahweh considered to be evil than anyone before him.' -1Kg 16

Ahab. Before we can really talk about Elijah, we must present our wayward King. Ahab is the 8th King of Israel since the nation broke away from Judah after the passing of King Solomon. He is the son of Omri, a military general who led a coup to take the throne. Omri and the six Kings before him passed in quick succession, giving Israel a rocky 58 years of initial leadership. Ahab will reign for 22 years, providing a measure stability for Israel.

But this political stability costs a great deal. For Ahab drinks down more perversity than all the previous Israeli Kings combined. A toxic culture has grown under his kingship that exceeds anything his apostate forefathers knew. It poisons everything. Darkness becomes the new normal.

How does Ahab create this spiritual swamp? To start with, Ahab promotes Baal worship into Israel. It has become all the rage among the who's who. His predecessor King Jeroboam's bull worship seems to have been just a warm-up for the spiritual cancer that is Baalism. It infects the land like an aggressive virus, twisting the hearts and minds of the people away from the God of their forefathers: Abraham, Isaac, and Jacob.

Our sinful sovereign also permits the worship of Asherah, Baal's female cohort. Worshipping this goddess and teaching her doctrines pumps petrol into an already sexually immoral furnace. Asherah is hailed as the enlightened Morning Star of Ancient Near Eastern mythology. But underneath her veneer of sophisticated education, Asherah worship is merely an excuse to get naked and worship idols.

Finally, there is the woman. Ahab is the first King since the ugly breakup with Judah to take a princess wife from a foreign, pagan king—an act forbidden by Scripture. We don't know why he got hitched to Princess Jezebel. Perhaps his successful father, King Omri, had arranged it. Perhaps he wedded her for the sake of political stability and economic opportunity with their seafaring and prosperous Phoenician neighbour. Domestically some commentators still remark that it was a great move. Having her as

Queen is an asset both politically and economically. Or perhaps Ahab married her because he thought she was pretty hot. You know, those Phoenician gals and stuff.

But whatever practical reasons may have influenced the decision, she is spiritually and morally whoreable. She drives the fake religion that entices Israel to prostitute itself with other gods. Ahab occupies himself with politics and the military well enough, but he abdicates his role as Defender of the Faith to someone who seeks to suffocate it entirely. She is the one who entices these rebellious Israelis to come even deeper under the cloud of Yahweh's righteous anger. Ahab may wear the crown, but Jezebel always seeks to wear the trousers. The King is not a man of strong spiritual conviction and is therefore easily blown about by emotional and sexual winds—a trait Jezebel can easily manipulate those to suit her purposes.

Ahab is ultimately culpable for this whole mess of course. He allows it on his watch. He fails to give godly leadership to both his Kingdom and his wife. Jezebel may be the active one but, as Pontius Pilate will learn centuries later, a leader cannot cleanse his hands of blood nor delegate culpability.

God does give him time to repent. God loves Ahab. He loves him enough to send him a mighty prophet to try to turn his heart. Men, you will shape the culture of your generation and the foundation of the generations to come. But how will you do so? The way you worship God matters. How you exercise self-control over your sexual and other appetites matter. If you allow lechery to live in you, it will be like a parasite that demands you feed it every day. You will be a slave to lust as Ahab was to Jezebel.

If you do marry, the woman whom you choose to take matters. We are not islands. Choices that we think of as being private are the ones that shape our character. Even our laziness and passivity has an effect on those around us. By contrast, the battles we fight in private for personal godliness prepare us to bring something of value to the public sphere.

Our King makes bad choices in his personal life and his name will be forever carved on the stones of history for leading Israel into the foulest apostasy. He fails to worship the Creator God in his prayer closet and so falters in leading the nation righteously. This all happens because he allows himself to be ruled by seduction rather than conviction.

What will future generations say of us? Will we be seen as sons of Ahab?

3

A Snapshot: Jezebel

'Ahab married Jezebel, then he proceeded to worship Baal.' -1Kg 16

Queen Jezebel is a Baal-snogging, fake-teaching, pride-marching, man-manipulating, Yahweh-blaspheming, prophets' blood-drinking monstrosity of a female.

And that's being nice.

This daughter of Ethbaal, the Phoenician King, grows up surrounded by power, education, luxury, and evil. Of course, she doesn't think of it as evil. No one sees their culture's sins for what they are. It is like air to a child or water to a fish: it's so much a part of us that we don't even know it is there. She thinks her culture is the rule by which others should be measured. Yes, Israel is used to being surrounded by pagan neighbours and their debauched royalty. But now we have a problem. The problem is that this ghoulish gal now has a throne in the midst of God's holy nation. It's one thing for a boat to be in the sea. It's quite another thing for the sea to be in the boat. And the nation is taking in wickedness of titanic proportions.

When Jezebel is given in marriage to the King of Israel, she probably has mixed feelings. Yes, it is good to marry a king. Perhaps not all of her sisters will manage to do so. But compared to her home city of Tyre, Samaria is a backwards, uneducated, hillbilly town. *'Have you seen how tiny the shopping street is?!'* and *'Can you even get good coffee in this place?!'* may have been some of her first reactions.

But this royal immigrant is not a passive woman. She is strong and active—a woman of great initiative. Of course, if a queen—or any woman—has a holy heart, her initiatives may mostly bear good fruit. But Jezebel's heart houses the vomitus stench of all that is unholy. Yes, she may have thought her intentions were good. But even wicked people do what is right in their own eyes. History is filled with unspeakable evils birthed by the good intentions of hearts not governed by the fear of the Lord.

Jezebel has a vision for herself and she won't let being married to a petulant and uncouth beta-king stop her. She will break glass ceilings and glass steeples. Our deviant diva will go where no Israeli queen has gone before. Her vision is to be this nation's reformer and bring it to a place of greater spiritual enlightenment and sexual liberation. Her colourful and savvy gods of Baal and Asherah will not just be the deities she worships in private palace quarters. No. They will be set up as the new saviours of Israel. Promises of power, potency, and fertility will be the draw for the Israeli men and women. Charm and mystery will be the atmosphere of worship. Orgasm will be the sacrament.

She may have spoken of being open-minded and tolerant as a ruler before taking the throne. Evil often speaks of minority rights as long as it is a minority. But behind all the talk of equality is masked the animal drive for power. And once securely in power, Jezebel seeks to eliminate everything opposed to her teaching. The biggest obstacle to this lascivious legislation is the worship of Yahweh. She imports and trains nearly one thousand priest-magicians to police religious expression. With her own private army established, she puts on her makeup, smiles coyly, and begins to eat righteous men like air.

This is the historical norm. Whenever evil gets the influence it craves, it then proceeds to silence the good. Jezebel is a real, historical woman. But she is not a one-off. The dynamic that she embodies makes several cameos throughout scripture and history. We see her corruption in the days of Malachi and her qualities in the Galilean lady Herodias, as she seeks to destroy John the Baptist. Peter warns us in his second epistle of sensual heresies that are thoroughly Jezebellic in nature and we see her subverting what is good at the church at Thyatira as she leads God's people into fake worship and immorality.

The Bible also ends with a vision of a world system described as a cataclysmic call girl who silences prophets and leads the nations into wrong religion and suicidal sex. This spiritual seductress does so by giving them spiked wine to drink, causing the nations to see themselves as enlightened, tolerant, and progressive as they follow her teaching. It is only later that the terror falls. Wherever in history this phantom appears, she comforts and kisses the brokenness of men; then she crumples their spirits like rubbish in the dustbins of their own souls.

We Ahab Men love Jezebel—if *love* is the right word. We certainly love ourselves through her. We eat up her smiles and her lies. She is bubble-wrapped candy floss with death at its heart. She numbs us to the emptiness of our own souls. In a sense, it is not that Jezebel is our ultimate problem. She is the fake solution to our problem. She makes us feel great about ourselves—but her potions only grow the shadows we carry within.

She is present in our 21st Century whenever Christians are seduced by her pornography. It is then that they slowly begin to lose their spiritual conviction and boldness to speak. No surprise. It's hard to wage war on demons with your trousers around your ankles.

Jezebel wields words of intimidation to silence those men who try to call us to holiness and repentance—especially repentance from sexual sin. Within our generation, she has castrated many of God's would-be spokesmen with the scissors of intimidation. She marches at the head of an aggressive army as Queen JezebeLGBT having people fined or fired from their jobs for failing to bow the knee to her sexual and spiritual dogmas.

And she is after you. She wants you to be a spiritually impotent Ahab Man devoid of character, resolve, and backbone. Yes, you will dance. But only as her marionette.

Before a reformer can tear down Jezebel's Baals and Asherahs in the world around him, he must first demolish them in his own heart. Any man who claims to be 'Protestant' but who fails to protest Jezebellic corruption in his own soul is a fraud. For it's in our personal areas of corruption that all holy protesting must begin. For every man is a potential Ahab—and Jezebel seeks to play us all.

Ahab Generation

'It's during Ahab's reign that Hiel rebuilt Jericho. He laid its foundations at the cost of his firstborn son Abiram, and he set up its gates at the cost of his youngest son Segub. This was according to the word of Yahweh spoken by Joshua son of Nun.' -1Kg 16

Once upon a midnight dreary, as churches stumbled weak and weary, and revivals seemed naught but old, forgotten lore. While monks nodded, nearly napping, suddenly there came a rapping, as if someone firmly hammering, hammering on Wittenberg's door…

Excuse the parody of Poe's immortal *The Raven*. The poem is a work of genius and my brutish hands tremble to tamper with it. I only dare do so because the darkness and vexation described in the poem capture well the spiritual gloom of the generation that Martin Luther was born into. Though this poem is only 173 years old, it is now 500 years since Luther hammered his 95 theses to the door of Wittenberg to protest the spiritual corruption of his day. In this sense, Luther lived at a time not wholly dissimilar to that of Elijah. He lived at a time when the surrounding social and religious culture had fallen to great depths of perversion: indulgences were sold, priests kept concubines, and Rome was a city flooded with greedy charlatans.

Not all cultures are equal. Some are worse than others. And Ahab's generation contains a culture that is among the most abominable in history. Canaanite worship had been slowly sneaking into Israeli culture for many years before Ahab arrived, but Yahwehism was still present—even if not all Israelis were deeply devoted to their nation's God. It is now Ahab and Jezebel that shepherd God's people from the strange fields of religious pluralism to the harsh desert sands of pagan totalitarianism.

And it isn't too hard to transition the people. Sadly, what is good in Israel is also weak. Jezebel brings money with her from Tyre. There is food on the table. Plus, the worship of these gods is relaxed compared to the strict ethics of Yahweh. Who cares too much if laws against the worship of Yahweh are being slowly introduced? People have always been willing to trade freedom of worship and expression for security, a good economy, and sexual license.

To show how spiritually weak and ready for takeover Israel is, the author of Kings gives us an example of the cultural attitude towards God's word.

Joshua, the great general of God's people, had spoken a curse when he watched Yahweh throw down the walls of the perverse city of Jericho. It was not just his word that Joshua uttered, it was God's word. The city was simply not to be rebuilt. But Israel is in something akin to a cold war with its southern neighbour of Judah. Ahab's Ministry of Defence thinks it strategic to have a fortified city there, so they give the contract to Hiel and his company gets to work in the rebuilding of the ancient city.

We do not know the details of how his sons die. We simply read that it is connected to the curse God placed on the city. But what we can know from this example is that this generation is one that openly defies God's word—there is no secret closet about it. What in previous generations was done quietly, now parades itself proudly. There is no more blushing. Guilt is forbidden. Perhaps when Hiel's sons died, it momentarily brought about the memory of Joshua's curse to Ahab's mind. Perhaps his heartfelt the fear of the Lord for a day. But by the next, it was back to business as usual.

Open and celebratory defiance of God's law is the mood in Ahab's Israel. And this is what makes them ready for a revival. But not a revival of repentance. It is a revival of paganism—a movement fuelled by a horny spirit, not the Holy Spirit.

Israel celebrates wickedness because the Fear of Yahweh is now dead in the lives of her people. This lax attitude towards holiness is what prepares the way for Jezebel's totalitarianism. No one trembles before God's word any longer. Those left in Israel who still identify as worshippers of Yahweh only do so half-heartedly. They carry a loyalty is largely sentimental.

And what of our nation? What of Britain or America? There was a time in Britain when the national, Anglican church was seen as a chaplain that comforted the people and held hands with those in power. But our generation no longer pretends to be Christian in any meaningful sense. Such generations do not need chaplains. They need missionaries whose gospel proclamation will pierce their consciences like a nail piercing the wood of an old university door.

And what condition is our church in? Are we a church fit for mission? Among the professed people of God, are there those who glory in sins that previous generations would have been ashamed to talk about? Not that previous generations didn't struggle with the same temptations of spirit and flesh that we do. They did. But what was their reaction to such struggles? Not a parade. It is the sons of Ahab who make excuses for sin with a theological and moral vocabulary that permits people to live contrary to God's law without blushing. Like the surrounding culture, we need far more than mere cheery chaplains. We do not need the homiletical equivalent of a cup of warm milk before bed. We need to be awakened to our condition.

And in ancient Israel, it is to awaken God's people to their true condition and to restore holiness that God raises up the witch-queen's antithesis: a prophet of fire whose voice will cut through the corrupt atmosphere like a raven's cry in the desert.

The Church is looking for better methods.
God is looking for better men.

-EM Bounds c.1890

#ElijahMen

It Begins: Elijah

'Elijah said to Ahab…' -1Kg 17

He ends his prayer, lifts his head, and stands. The sweat from his exertion kisses the cool mountain air as he surveys the familiar hills all around. He knows today is the day. Today he goes to the city.

The city. Samaria. Geographically, it is only 30 miles and one river crossing away. But it may as well be 3,000 miles and an ocean away. The city is where the educated, religious, and political elite play their polished games. And, as a man from the rugged terrain of Gilead, it isn't really his vibe. He doesn't do polished very well. Even his wardrobe places him apart from the posh urbanites. His rough camel hair tunic and old leather belt contrast sharply with the latest designer threads brought straight to the Samarian top shops from the boats that dock in Tyre's port. As a Gileadite, he doesn't do dandyism. Elijah isn't your model metrosexual.

The Prophet sets out. He has been given a message from the Heavenly King to announce to the man who now sits on Israel's throne. How will he say it? He's never been talkative or given to clever wordsmithery. Just how does one throw down the gauntlet and tell the royals that their darling Baal is fake deity? Might as well stick with the direct approach. *Your impotent rain god has about as much chance of rescuing you from Yahweh's coming drought as I do of winning the Miss Israeli Beauty contest. Crops will turn to dust, the economy will falter, and people will die. So, um, no more rain.*

'Until when did you say?'

Until I say otherwise.

'Oh.'

When Elijah started praying, he probably didn't know that God would draft him to be a spokesman as well. Our crowd-averse desert preacher may well have experienced a similar reluctance to Moses when God sent him from looking after sheep in the wilderness to stand in the courts of a cruel Pharaoh and deliver an equally unwelcomed message.

We are born cowards. To be truly courageous, we must be born again. Elijah trembles before God. Men who do so rarely tremble before other men—even before a king who holds the power of death in his command. The fear of God is what makes Elijah fearless.

It is of great importance that we speak to humanity about God. But it is of even greater importance that we speak to God about humanity. Not every man who grieves over the damnables of his generation is sent to speak to politicians or vast crowds. But it is certain that when God does choose a man to speak publicly, he chooses from amongst those who howl before Him privately.

Centuries later the half-brother of this world's Saviour sums up the life of Elijah in two words: *he prayed*. Everything else that he does is a footnote to, and an expounding of that. Before our prophet is anything in public, he is much in private. And after crying out many words to the God of Israel, he's now been given one from Him—one to execute before the reckless ruler and his poisonous princess bride. This rustic son of the sands now hikes to the capital with a divine word that will soon be the talk of all who dwell in the Samarian halls of power.

Somewhere in the secret places, on a mountain or in plain, he had been alone with God, an intercessor against the debasing idolatry of Ahab.

-EM Bounds

#ElijahMen

Angry God

*Ahab did more to provoke the Lord God of Israel to anger
than all the Kings of Israel that were before him.* -1Kg 16

Does God get angry? Elijah's epic makes no sense if we cannot answer this question correctly. And not just in regards to these few canonical chapters; the whole Biblical narrative makes no sense if we are uncertain on this point. Our narrator describes God's anger as laying upon Israel like a dark fog when Elijah steps onto the scene. But it is this concept of divine wrath that our generation doesn't do particularly well with.

It shouldn't be surprising that a generation finds certain elements of God's character challenging to comprehend. After all, He is wide, expansive, and whole. We are products of cultures that are small, narrow, and broken. We may struggle to see how seemingly contradictory attributes can exist within one integrated being. But our difficulty reconciling certain passages has more to do with us and our lack of imagination than it does with Him.

When the gospel first came to these British Isles, it wasn't the revelation of God's retributive anger that troubled our ancestors. Rather, the Angles and Saxons stumbled over the concept of God's forgiveness. In their honour oriented society, forgiveness just didn't make any sense. Ironically, it is precisely that same forgiveness that our generation gravitates towards as a concept. Paul writes that we should *'consider the kindness and severity of God.'* He instructs us to do so because he knows our tendency is to focus on just his kindness or just his severity—depending on our personality or culture.

God is pissed at sin. All sin committed is primarily against our Creator who designed us to live for Him. As the medieval rabbi Rashi wrote, *'As long as idolatry exists in the world, God's fierce anger will exist in the world.'* But as a people, who have had the light of Scripture, turn from the truth and increase their idolatry, so does that anger likewise increase. And few generations have rejected God's purposes like Ahab's. His vengeance now rightly reaches the boiling point. One can almost imagine the stench of sin bruising the nostrils of holy angels who veer too close above the nation.

14

We'll never understand God's patience and mercy if we don't first understand His wrath. It is not difficult to show patience to a person who doesn't anger us. It is those who stir us to anger that we must exercise self-control with. In the same way, it is because sin angers God so much, that we can be amazed at his patience in holding back the judgement we deserve. A god who never gets angry can never be said to be patient.

What does it cost a God who doesn't hate evil to show mercy? Nothing. It's only when we see the enormity of God's righteous judgement against us, that his mercy becomes truly merciful. This is what gives the message of Jesus's blood its power. This is what causes a contrite man to leap up and sing, *'Amazing grace, how sweet the sound, that saved a wretch like me!'*

Even in our agnostic generation, the default thought of many is that, if there is a God, He is love. It is revealing that we presume this love. We do this to such a degree that it is unclear if we mean *'God is love'* or if we mean *'Love is God'*—which is quite different. In presuming His love and kindness, we rob it of its power to transform. Can anyone logically explain why, if there is a God, He would have any inclination to love something as royally screwed up as the human race? No, it makes no sense. Yet here we are presuming that if God doesn't lovingly affirm every aspect of our lives, He has somehow done something terribly wrong. *Shame on Him.*

Difficult as it is for us to grasp, this doctrine is revealed from Genesis to Revelation. It has been a key part of church teaching for 2,000 years. Many whimsically quip that *'all roads lead to God.'* That may be. But many of those roads lead to Him as Judge. Only through Jesus can we meet God as Father.

God's judgement is especially clear in our reading of Ahab and Elijah. God's violence against Israel has been building like water against a dam wall for over 50 years. This wall is God's patience. Ahab then does more to add to that anger than all previous Kings combined. It is now ready to burst. Israel has become a spiritual stench—and justice demands that God wipe it out. It is approaching its Sodom moment.

Into this condemned culture, Elijah ventures on a mission of mercy. He aches to see his nation turn back to the Holy One of Israel. His prayers—along with the cries of other prophets and righteous people—have been building up another dam. But this dam is not holding back a reserve of righteous retribution. This one is storing up a flood of repentance, revival, and reformation. Only time will tell which wall breaks first.

The Word of the LORD

'The word of Yahweh came to Elijah... and he obeyed the word of Yahweh.' -1Kg 17

Elijah delivers God's message to the King and his sultry sorceress. The rain ceases. The crops begin to wilt and this nation whose GDP is based on agriculture and the herding of animals slips into recession and then depression. This singular word from Elijah starves the nation's economy and we see in the physical what has long been the case in the spiritual—a famine of food follows a famine of God's word.

At the risk of oversimplifying the matter, the reason so many churches in our country are withering is that we also have a famine of God's word. It's not the only factor, but a large one. Few people in our nation attend church the way so many did in our grandparent's day—much less are active participants. Often, many go out of habit and to see friends. They no longer go to church with the expectancy that God will speak with divine power and cut their spirit and soul asunder (Heb. 4). When God speaks, people are shaken and they leave different to when they came in.

In the book of Ruth, we are told of another famine that happened in Israel, long before Elijah's day. In a sad twist of irony, Naomi and her family had to leave Bethlehem (Heb: *the house of bread*), because there was no bread there. Is it much different in many churches today? The church is to be God's bakery. But all too often we put on a show that makes reference to bread, without actually delivering bread. Hungry people arrive and go through the motions of a service—be it traditional or modern—an stroll out without having their hearts pierced through with a word from heaven.

Elijah possesses this sword—a blade more powerful than all of Ahab's armies. But before he could wield it, he first had to receive it in prayer and needed to be transformed by it. This is why, when he stands before Ahab, he says that it will not rain, *'by my word'*. It is written of Elijah that, *'he obeyed the word of Yahweh.'* Do not seek after God's word if your heart is not set to obey it.

Centuries later, when tempted in the desert, the incarnate Christ will respond to Satan's temptation of making stones into bread by quoting from Deuteronomy, '*Man shall not live by bread alone, but by every word that proceeds from the mouth of the Lord.*' If Jesus will need to take time away from distractions in order to feast upon God's word, how much more do we? Before Jesus will start preaching the word, he will feast upon it—and he'll season his spiritual feasting with fasting.

Many say they are followers of Jesus. But what does that mean? How many of today's hip young preachers and bloggers will fast for 40 days away from distractions just to meditate on the book of Deuteronomy? (All of Jesus' quotes in the desert were from this majestic book.) We're too busy sorting out our coffee and thinking up the best social media updates to impress the crowds. As a result, we may put on an exciting show. The band is stylish, the preacher says something funny or profound. Everyone has a buzz.

Except for God.

It may be that a preacher or write feasts upon theology books, but fails to feed the flock. If he feasts on God's word, he will always have something to give. Theology books can stimulate the intellect and make you feel proud that you've become so smart. Being smart isn't wrong. There are no heavenly awards given for being a dummy. But we can have a giant brain and still have a tiny heart. God's word is living—something that destroys pride and demands transformation.

In a way, our time is more tragic than Elijah's or Luther's. In Luther's day, there was a famine of God's word because the existing authorities wouldn't allow the Scriptures to be translated from Latin into the language of the people. Luther protested by translating them into German and giving them out anyway. The Pope sought to stop this by burning every German Bible his forces could find. But in our day, the devil doesn't have to do anything quite so dramatic. He doesn't care about burning Bibles. Christians barely read the ones they have. Our famine is caused by distractions, not dictators.

Elijah shatters the spiritual coma of the country by delivering God's word. But he's not off to do a book tour now or sign any autographs. He's getting alone with God to receive from him. It will be three years before he speaks again.

The secret of Elijah's praying and the character of the man are found in the words, 'Before whom I stand.'

-EM Bounds

Before the King

'As the Lord God of Israel lives, before whom I stand' -1Kg 17

How is Elijah received at court? Is the King angry? Is Elijah seen as a threat? Does the King yell at his guards to seize the prophet after he delivers his prophetic word? Does someone throw a spear at him and does he barely escape with his life? Or, is he laughed at? Who is this man who appears out of the caves with Ben Kenobi like mystery? Does the court assume that this man who claims to have power over the weather is drunk? Whatever the first impressions may have been, in the months to come the court will certainly remember with pointed discomfort the words spoken by that strange Gileadite who stood so boldly before their King.

We all stand before someone or something. We wake up each morning with a circumstance or a person on our mind—a reference point that helps define who we are and how we act and react to the world around us. It is something we want, something we love, or something we fear to lose. Elijah is physically standing before the throne of Ahab, the most powerful man in his country. This King commands armies and possesses the authority to have the prophet swiftly executed. Most of us would wet ourselves.

But Elijah isn't fazed. How? He has more than strong coffee flowing through him. His power comes, not from what he drinks, but from what he sees. He has eyes of faith that have been cultivated by unseen hours spent in the secret place. He sees two thrones. He sees Ahab's seat for what it is: a brief and fleeting thing. Beyond that, he sees the high and fiery throne that reigns forever unmoved in the granite halls of eternity. It is before that throne that Elijah trembles in private—and now he can stand in public. Elijah is not unique among the men of God in this regard. It is by faith that Mordecai will also stand centuries later before the wicked Haman—while everyone else pleads with him to bow.

Such a vision causes a man to fly the flag of holiness over his life. Sadly, the words 'holiness' and 'worldliness' have all but disappeared from 21st Century Christian speak here in the UK. These nouns get in the way of us showing trendy unbelievers just how hip we (think we) are. But when we live with a vision of the eternal throne, our goals change. There is only One we want to please. Only His opinion matters. This causes us to get rid of the compromise in our own lives and therefore fit to confront the spiritual plagues at work in the church and society.

True holiness leads to remarkable courage. Solomon wrote that '*The righteous are as bold as lions*'. But the devil uses intimidation to silence God's men by making them eager for culture's approval and fearing it's angry rejection. If Jezebel cannot get you to celebrate fake teaching, she will at least try to silence you from speaking His truth. When we tremble before God, we march in courage towards men. The more we bend the knee before the true King, the less influence bullies and manipulators will wield over us. If we are to stand and speak for God in our generation, we cannot fear what those around us fear. Our lives must be controlled by a divine fear that leaves every earthly intimidation toothless.

This World's God

'As the LORD, God of Israel lives, before whom I stand.' -1Kg 17

Does the devil rule our generation?

Read what Elijah says. Ahab and Jezebel have led Israel into the dark jungle of idolatry. They did so with greater zeal than any of the Kings before them. Baal and Asherah are now worshipped in the field and in the temple. Paganism has displaced Yahweh worship as the chief moral, social, political, and religious power in the land. The people are as eager to go to hell as American women are for their pumpkin-spiced lattes in the autumn.

And yet, Elijah still sees and proclaims Yahweh to be Israel's God.

How can he do this? He is not blind to the situation. There are no rose-tinted glasses being worn by our prophet. He knows that society no longer maintains any of the spiritual or sexual values that flow from God's Law.

Elijah is woke. He knows his age is apostate. Like Heaven's God, he too smells the vomitus reek of incense being offered up to other deities in the name of progress and enlightened thinking. Yet, he looks at the land and still can say, *'The LORD is God here.'*

How can an honest man say such a thing?

Jesus speaks of the evil one as *'the prince of this world'* (John 14.30). He knows that men and women love darkness, and that wickedness is the natural spiritual, moral, and sexual condition of humanity. We are influenced by the dark prince more than our Creator. Ours has been a rebellious planet from the beginning. It should not be so.

'But now God calls all men everywhere to repent' (Acts 17). God is King, and the wicked prince is leading humanity in a revolution against Him. Ahab and Jezebel are tools of this prince just like many of those in the halls of culture, politics, and religion are in our generation. As Christians, we are the counter-revolutionaries. We are to be God's antithesis to the ways of Jezebel. We confront her ghastly Baalism with a godly Biblicism. We seek to persuade everyone back to the King who created us. He is kind and has made provision for the forgiveness of even the most rebellious. Men and

21

women are invited to surrender without fear of receiving the punishment their rebellion merits.

This is why the King has not decisively stepped in yet: He's giving us a chance to repent and come back home. To speak for God in our day, we must have the conviction that everyone will be called to give an account before Him. The rebellion will not go on forever. It cannot. Yes, we preach the gospel humbly—aware of our own capacity for rebellion against God. But we're not wimpy about it either. Everyone *should* repent and faithfully serve the King. Our call to the world is to lay down its futile weapons and surrender. Baal is defeated and it is only fitting his soldiers put up the white flag.

Obedience in Hiding

'Go and hide.' -1Kg 17

Elijah goes viral. The thing all politicians—and far too many preachers—dream will happen. Out of nowhere, this nobody from nowhere is cast onto the national stage. His brief and bold word breaks the internet. The pundits talk about nothing but him. *What will be his next big venture? How will he follow up on this ministry success? How will he grow and maintain his platform now that he is in such a place of prominence? Can we get him on our show? An interview perhaps?* But there's a problem. No one can find him.

There is a death to self that needs to happen before we preach. Some may disapprove of the message we write or speak, even strongly so. It takes courage to utter a word contrary to a militant zeitgeist and a compromised religious system. Being willing to face such opposition is obedience.

But there is another test. Another death must happen after we speak. Those who would speak for Yahweh in this generation must also know how to follow his Spirit into hiding. Prominence can become addictive even if it's a prominence of opposition. You will have enemies but you also have people cheering you on. Your sinful nature can begin to crave the prophetic spotlight. You used to be an unknown. Now you're hailed as a reformer.

And your spiritual pride stinks to God. To prevent this pride from taking over the hearts of God's revivalists and reformers, he tells them, *'Go hide yourself'*. Often that whisper will come at the most inconvenient times when it seems counter-intuitive or when it seems that momentum is just building.

But Elijah obeys. He forgoes the book deal. Now all this seems like wasted time to human eyes. It's not to God. Elijah is learning to live for an audience of One—and is strengthened by meat brought by ravens. During these three years, he doesn't speak to masses. He develops an unusual friendship with a foreigner that leads to her salvation and his faith grows to mountainous proportions. God is preparing him for a confrontation that will shake the powers of darkness like a wild dog shakes a rat.

If only I could pray the way that dog looks at meat.

-Martin Luther

#ElijahMen

Elijah Men Eat Meat

'Ravens brought him bread and meat in the morning and in the evening.' -1Kg 17

Elijah unleashes his prophetic message upon the unsuspecting King. The fulfillment of this short, singular word will do more to upset Ahab's political-economic agenda than all the internal pundits and foreign powers combined. God now tells Elijah to hide.

He gets out of the public view and eats meat brought to him by ravens. A few scholars have argued that the Hebrew word translated as 'ravens' may be a reference to a particular Arabic group. So, it could've been Arabs that were giving this Israeli man some food. (Which some may cheekily quip is an even greater miracle.) But the vast majority of scholars say that it is indeed the large, glossy black bird scavenger bird that can be found the world over.

Ravens get a few privileged mentions in the Bible. The first is in Genesis with Noah who sends one out as the first bird to go scouting. The last is in Luke's Gospel where Jesus says that God cares for and feeds ravens. But it is their size—considerably larger than crows—that make them especially suited for bringing Elijah hunks of meat.

It may seem that Elijah is glamping at first glance. Having meat delivered to your tent (or whatever little shelter he was able to put together by the wadi) sounds like quite a luxury. But we must assume that the ravens weren't bringing him already cooked, perfectly seasoned rib-eye steaks. Ravens are scavengers. Think road kill. But that's not a problem. Elijah is a man and he doesn't mind skinning his own animals and cooking up whatever the birds bring. This is about sustenance and nutrition, not luxury. Ravens are sent to fill a ravenous appetite. It is important that Elijah eats all this meat. He is not yet done his mission and he needs strength for his upcoming confrontations with Baal and Asherah.

To be a man, you must eat meat.

Now before I get attacked by a nightmarish mob of androgynous Vegans, I will concede a couple of things. First of all, yes, girls should also eat meat too. A woman who can kill and butcher her own food has a particular aura of beauty to the discerning eye. I will also concede that Elijah doesn't just eat meat nor is he strictly on a paleo diet. He eats bread with the meat (steak sandwich?) and later on in the same chapter we find Elijah eating cake. Now I'm tempted to think this cake thing is an effeminate backsliding on his part, but God seems to sanction it and he eats cake yet again in chapter 19. Thankfully, by the end of that chapter, we see Elijah eating a mountain of beef. Our carnivorous man has returned to his senses and all is right with the world.

What does all this have to do with us other than being a great excuse to grill up some ribs and bacon tonight? The author of Hebrews chides his readers for their immaturity. He says they still are on a diet of milk when they should be eating meat. He ends the chapter by saying *'But strong meat belongs to them that are of full age'* (5.14). He connects their spiritual maturity, not with the amount of time they've been Christians, but with their spiritual diet.

If you want to grow into a man that God can use, you must eat spiritual meat. Years passed do not make one strong in God. You will be unfit for confronting the idols of our day if you eat spiritual junk food. And this sugary, processed crap is everywhere. Just look at your social media newsfeed. Many of the comments and memes seem to be crafted by the zeitgeist of our age—and not by a particular human being with free thought. We're obese on spiritual junk food and unfit for God's mission. We need to discipline ourselves to consume spiritual protein. Spiritual maturity has always come by the exercise of obedience to God along and by eating nutrient dense spiritual food.

Have a plan to study God's word daily. Any plan is better than no plan. Plan, then do it. And don't stop there. Read Christian classics that have stood the test of generations and not the latest spiritual fake food from publishers hoping their latest book sells big. Get alone with God daily and nourish your soul on a grill of spiritual lamb chops and T-bones. Eat more spiritual protein than a bodybuilder eats soy and see how God will begin to use you. Our staying weak doesn't serve this world.

Is God a Misogynist?

*'Elijah took the child, and brought him down into the house,
and gave him to his mother.'* -1 Kg 17

A superficial understanding of Elijah could leave us under the illusion that he—or perhaps even the God who worked through Elijah—is a misogynist. Sadly, this term, in addition to being hard to spell, has become loaded, politicised, and increasingly vague. CS Lewis pointed out that when such things happen we are witnessing *verbicide*: the death of a word. It's a shame because misogyny and its counterpart misandry are both real things. So, let's define. By misogynist, we do NOT mean a man who despises a woman. We mean a man who despises a woman *because* she is a woman.

This, Elijah was not. Elijah stood against the work of the queer queen—but not because she was a woman or a foreigner. He resisted her plans because she was leading God's people into fake worship and immorality. Any man whose imagination is kindled by Elijah's zealous example should take note before he goes to battle.

Elijah's spiritual maturity is demonstrated by his dealings with one of Jezebel's old neighbours. The Cherith brook where Elijah hid evaporates into dust and God sends him to Zarephath to meet a woman. For those of us who are a bit rusty in our Ancient Near East geography, we need to not rush over this detail. God isn't sending him nearby for a bite to eat. He travels over 90 miles of mountainous terrain into another country. That would be a long drive, even a good a date. But this is no date, and he is not driving.

Most importantly of all, we need to note that this country is where Queen Jezebel is from. Ahab and Jezebel are undergoing an international search for Elijah all while God leads him to a village just 10 miles north of the cruel Queen's home city. God sends his premier prophet on a perilous journey - to show His love to a single gal who is not the most charming of cupcakes.

Now, some of the more prim and proper among us may raise our eyebrows that Elijah is going to be housemates with a woman. We might raise our eyebrows even higher to know that she is a pagan and of the same sexually immoral culture as Jezebel. But the most amazing thing during this time is Elijah's gracious behaviour with this sarcastic Sidonian. This same prophet who will call down the fires of judgement on proud Israeli soldiers undertakes a dangerous journey to humbly care for and minister to a Phoenician.

Elijah never speaks directly to Madame Jezebel. But in our reading of 1 Kings 17, we see him engaging in banter with his female friend. The miracles Elijah performs brings death to some in Israel. But with this young woman's child, he places him on his own bed and cries out to God for life to be restored. And it is. He seems to care tremendously for this woman and her young boy. And this care works. She starts off the narrative as jaded and cynical. But by the end, she is tenderly and gratefully professing faith in the God of Israel. May we never underestimate the transformative power of consistently showing love and care to even the hardest of hearts.

This sort of love is the big difference between true holiness and a man who simply has a judgmental spirit. Elijah may be gruff and unsophisticated, but he's not rude. Do the people you work with describe you as gracious and joyful? Do you bring life into your household? Before Elijah calls down fire from heaven, he must show that he's a blessing to live with.

A man is manifesting misogyny when he labels a woman with '*Jezebel spirit*' just because she disagrees with him or the relationship proves difficult. While this term does have a valid use in describing acts of manipulation, seduction, or cruelty, it should be used appropriately lest it suffers verbicide as well.

Instead of demonstrating misogyny, Elijah demonstrates one of the best, non-romantic, male-female relationships in all of Scripture. The man who confronts and slaughters Baal's prophets first patiently and caringly leads a foreigner to faith in Yahweh. Elijah is not a misogynist—nor is he a Feminist. Elijah is a friend.

Mission to Zarephath

'Get up, go to Zarephath that belongs to Sidon and stay there.' -1Kg 17

Elijah's mission to the foreign town of Zarephath is not a secondary episode. Rather, it gives essential perspective. Jesus cited this episode as having a parallel to his own, so we must get this. It is a key event that all potential reformers and revivalists must keep in mind or else they lose ultimate focus.

It is not enough to merely heal a wounded soldier. We must get him back onto the battlefield in fighting condition. It is not enough just to get the water out of the ship. We must get the ship back in the water and set it on its mission. Likewise, it is not enough merely to rid the church of fake teachers and immorality. We must keep our ultimate mission in view.

So let's talk mission. Let's assume that we accomplish our goal of Bible-slapping the Jezebellic zeitgeist out of the church. Great. Then what? What would we then do with ourselves? What is our mission?

The church's mission focus has been largely hijacked by the new regressives. For most of her history, the main mission of the church has been clearly understood: to preach the gospel and make obedient disciples of Jesus throughout the nations. But Satan has belched upon us a faux-guilt complex rooted in a dimly understood European colonial history. Somehow, we've believed the lie that sending preachers to other countries to proclaim the gospel is racist. How it is racist, we're not quite sure. But this is what the cool kids have told us and we have believed them. As the church was made for mission, we replace gospel advancement with other causes: recycling, opposing fracking, reducing carbon footprints, wealth distribution—or whatever the latest Guardian approved cause may be.

There are some Biblical churches that rightfully disregard these hellishly humanistic substitutes, but they then lose foreign mission as a focus because *'we have so many problems here at home.'* Given all the spiritual darkness that we see in Israel, it would be easy to assume that God might put foreign missions on hold. Elijah has no shortage of work to do within his national boundaries. After all, there are plenty of fake prophets to combat and plenty

29

of seduced hearts to turn. Yet, God sends Elijah to another nation to spend two years of his life witnessing to one pagan woman and her son. How does one even begin to evaluate whether that was a wise use of time and resources? Surely a gifted preacher and miracle worker like Elijah could be doing more important things? He could be preaching to huge crowds back in Israel, no? God doesn't seem to think so. He sends his premier prophet into foreign missions for a season.

Reformers can be so focused on awakening the church within their own locality that we forget the bigger call the Father has given us: to see Jesus exalted in all nations. This was a tendency among some Reformers 500 years ago. They were so focused on reforming the church's theology and ecclesiology that sending out missionaries into foreign lands was neglected.

It was 200 years later that Protestants began to gain a significant vision for global evangelism. When they did start, they did amazing work. The biographies of Hudson Taylor, William Carrey, Amy Carmichael, David Brainerd, etc., are now Christian classics worthy of every growing Christian's prayerful read. They didn't just go to do service projects either. They went to preach, baptize, and disciple.

Today, 2/3 of all Christians live in the third-world. There are more active disciples in Asia than in the United States, and more in Africa than in Europe. This global shift in Christianity is thanks to men and women who obeyed God's marching orders and gave their lives abroad just 200 years ago. In a beautiful (and ironic) turn, missionaries from countries that are poorer in material goods, but richer in God, are now coming to our cities and telling us Europeans that we need to repent. The bread we cast on the waters is returning to us. The POC (Primates of Colour) within third-world Anglicanism are the ones giving well-deserved rebuke to their (mostly) white ecclesiastical siblings who increasingly tolerate sexual immorality and fake teaching in their midst. Their voices are strong. May God help us listen.

The Father's goal is to see Jesus praised among the nations. Who is our widow? We may not be able to go abroad ourselves, but in today's world of instant communications and affordable travel, we can all connect with global missions in some way. There are practical ways anyone can get involved, and it doesn't take too long online to find groups that can point you in the right direction. We may rightfully desire to be a prophetic witness within our own church and nation, but what is our Zarephath?

Prophets and the Poor

'I'm collecting sticks to make some food so that my son and I may eat and die.' -1Kg 17

When Elijah meets the woman who will be his mission field for the next two years, we notice that she isn't exactly loaded with cash—a point that allows us to frolic about in the fun field of stereotypes for a minute. A superficial stereotype that one may hear, in the midst of our politicised culture, is that if a man is deeply concerned for personal and righteous morality, then he is probably indifferent to the needs of the poor or marginalised. This has come about because, though our Western societies have rejected Christian theology, we have not wholly abandoned a notion of Christian concern for the weak. But we no longer have a solid ideological framework to put this concern in. Europe now lives in a shattered and fragmented Christendom, so we end up with a society where things like personal righteousness and mercy towards the poor are often in opposition. This shouldn't be surprising. Only the Cross is able to hold all the Christian virtues together.

After Elijah deals a harsh word of judgement against a spiritually inept and immoral King, he spends three years in hiding during which time he cares for a widow and a fatherless boy—the very heart of Biblical social mercy. We have already talked about how it is significant that he had this relationship because she was a woman. But it is also significant that she was completely broke. He showed his sexual integrity in having a close but sexually pure relationship with her as a housemate. He also showed his financial integrity by providing (albeit supernaturally) for her and her son and eating the same food as they did.

With all the other craziness happening in the world, God chooses to provide through Elijah for a single widow and her boy. He is not too busy rebuking false prophets to get food for the hungry—and neither should we be. The New Testament Elijah, the Reverend Johnny Baptist, was of the same spirit. Yes, he rebuked sexual sin—he was cast into prison for that. But he also rebuked material greed and called *'those with two shirts, share with the person who has none.'*

31

James, whose epistle has a fiercely Elijah-like call to righteousness, also embrace social mercies. He specifically mentions Elijah in chapter five in regards to prayer and he probably also has Elijah in mind when he writes, *'Pure religion is to care for widows and orphans in their distress AND to keep yourself unspotted by the world'* (emphasis mine). We need to keep these twin responsibilities in mind as many Christians tend to follow society's lead and just gravitate towards one or the other. We pursue personal responsibility AND we care for the poor and marginalised. We do not need to abandon the first to obey the second.

We are aware of the sexual sin of Sodom and Gomorrah. In addition to the narrative of Genesis 19, Jude comments in his epistle that the Sodomites *'gave themselves to fornication and strange flesh'*. But these acts of immorality are not the whole story. Ezekiel also describes the spiritual environment that caused this sexual wickedness to flourish like a weed. He writes, *'Sodom and her daughters were arrogant, overfed, and unconcerned. They did not help the poor and needy.'* When we max out our financial means and don't share with those poorer than us, we create an environment where sexual perversion is more likely to grow. The discipline of generosity spills over into other areas where self-control is also needed. We call for repentance from immorality. We must also call for repentance from greed. The two are not disconnected.

Our wallet is closer to our genitalia than we realise.

If we had more of Elijah's praying, marvels would not be the marvels they are now to us... Everything is tame and feeble because our praying is tame and feeble.

-EM Bounds

#ElijahMen

Prayer that Raises the Dead

'And he stretched himself upon the child three times, and cried unto the Lord... and the LORD heard the voice of Elijah.' -1Kg 17

Elijah is dealt an unexpected blow. The young mother that he had blessed is now facing an unspeakable curse: the death of her little boy.

Now Elijah knows a God who can redeem from the very worst of circumstances. But this redemption is not going to be brought down from heaven on the careless wings of half-hearted praying. Elijah doesn't merely look at the boy, shrug his shoulders and mutter *'Well if it's your will God...'*. No, none of that impotent praying will do the trick.

Rather, he takes the dead boy and brings him into his own bed. He makes this personal. He stretches himself out upon the boy. He identifies with him. He takes this boy's death as if it were his very own. He does it three times. He persists. His faith will not be turned away by a lack of answer the first two times. Three times he stretches himself out in crying out for life. His praying transcends earthly boundaries and raids heaven to call upon a grace greater than death.

Elijah's voice is heard. God sends life back into the boy. Not only is the boy raised to life, the mother finds an eternal life that cannot be taken away from her. Elijah had built a relationship with a woman who did not share his faith. He had blessed her with bread and she was grateful. But it was in seeing her boy raised that she came to personal faith. The heathen gal has not just been blessed, she has been properly converted.

Do we pray just to pray? Is it a mere exercise or form of personal meditation? Or do we pray in order to be heard? Few of our churches gather to pray anymore. Among those that do, prayer is sometimes presented as a creative hobby or as a way to help a person become more 'spiritual'. *How to grow in the art of intercession*, the pamphlet to the seminar may advertise. But prayer is an art only in the sense that war is an art. It is an aggressive cry raised to God to come down and shake a demon-filled world. Prayer that calls down the Kingdom is not for the curious, but for the desperate. Prayer gatherings of desperate people are few and far between now in Britain, but any true reformation must begin as a reformation of prayer.

Churches do many activities that their wider communities benefit from. Christians have started countless soup kitchens, hospitals, and orphanages during the last 2,000 years. We've done so much of it, that society now expects it of us. Feeding the poor gives moral validation to the message of a God who generously and freely gives to those who are spiritually poor. This will soften some hearts. It makes some people appreciative and can give us a hearing. But charity programs are not listed as one of the *'signs that shall follow those that believe.'* We can do such things without an ounce of supernatural help.

Some things simply will not happen until we learn how to pray in such a way that causes us to be heard. How many of us can say to an unbelieving world when it faces tragedy, *'Give me your son'*? How many of us are willing to risk such embarrassment? Are we willing to risk our image for God's glory? We often say our prayers, but do we really pray? Those who are willing to be broken in prayer are the ones who will break hellish fortresses.

Power in circumstances such as Elijah faced comes from long hours spent alone with God. It's not cultivated by praying with one eye on heaven and the other checking how many likes our last social media post got. It comes when we learn to pray specific prayers about issues in real space and real time.

Elijah and the Hate Preachers

Elijah stretched himself over the boy and cried,
'Oh LORD, let this child live!' -1Kg 17

We live in a world where it can be difficult to discern the voice of a prophet who hates sin from the voice of preacher who hates sinners. But from Heaven's perspective, these two characters are as dissimilar as the East and the West. But our culture rarely distinguishes between despising what a man does and despising who a man is.

Elijah could be severe. He could be violent. He slew the prophets of Baal and called down fire on God's enemies. But he was not driven by hate. He was not immaturely making denunciations of others who had personally hurt him. He didn't want Ahab to die. Elijah wanted him to repent from the influence of Jezebel and be redeemed.

And it's that ultimate goal of redemption that separates the words of a piercing prophetic voice from that of a hate preacher. Before a prophet's words whip anyone, he first weeps over them in the private place of prayer. His words may be hard, but his heart is soft.

Those who have a heart to please God can tell the difference between a strong prophetic voice that is willing to speak what is unpopular and mere hate speech. Yes, both the true prophet and the hate preacher may speak against something that is wrong. But that's where the similarities stop.

True prophets lose sleep praying down mercy upon those they preach to. Hate preachers lose no sleep over the fate of those they denounce. True prophets weep as they call the lost to turn from their sin. Hate preachers enjoy condemning the lost in their sin whether they turn or not. True prophets are quick to listen and slow to speak. Hate preachers are quick to speak and slow to listen.

True prophets tremble at the enormity of their own sin. Hate preachers believe their own sin is small compared to others. True prophets can speak to a valley of dry bones and see a righteous army raised up. Hate preachers, with a self-righteous spirit, simply tell the bones how dry they are.

True prophets take no joy in the attention (negative or positive) their words may bring - they prefer to be alone with God. Hate preachers seem to thrive on the attention their words bring them.

The church does not need self-righteous, hate-filled preachers. Nor does it need silent leaders who side step or compromise on important issues from the platform. We need those who can pray and speak in the compassion and courage of an Elijah. We need this because Elijah points us to Jesus. His cross is a message of both offensive truth and radical love.

Jesus' death speaks the hard truth that you are so wicked and evil that the perfect Son of God had to be crucified in order to save you. At the same time, it speaks a message of unspeakable love: that God so cared for you that He was willing to leave heaven to do so.

A true revival means nothing less than a revolution, casting out the spirit of worldliness and selfishness, and making God and His love triumph in the heart and life.

- Andrew Murray

Goodbye to Her, Hello to Destiny

'After three years, God told Elijah to go to Ahab.' -1Kg 18

He's leaving her today. He's sure of that. After all, there's another woman in the picture. And that woman is trouble. He may be wondering how his housemate will react. But he knows he must move on. God told him to. The coming confrontation could get a bit messy and he wouldn't want her or the boy to get caught in the crossfire. Elijah will go without human companionship into the eye of the storm. Men of God are built for messy confrontations.

Elijah begins the walk to Northern Israel. His faith is strong. He remembers how God has provided for him over the last three years: 600 meals from the mouths of ravens and 1000 meals from the same bag of flour. A life of seeing these small miracles gives him no doubt that God will perform the big miracle on the mountain.

If he's wrong, he will be executed by the authorities at once. But if God does what He promised, then his years of petitioning heaven for revival and reformation may finally receive their answer. The heart of Ahab and the people of his nation will be freed from Jezebel's deceit and turned back to the God of their fathers. This is his destiny.

Will he see the woman and her son again? He doesn't know. Perhaps not in this life. But he must say goodbye to what is good, in order to embrace what is best. He cannot cling to the people God has given him more than to the God who gave them. For the sake of the call, many of God's men in the centuries to come will also have to say goodbye to their friends and commit their affections to heaven.

Admittedly, we don't know for sure what this woman and her son meant to Elijah. We can only speculate and attempt to read between the lines about what went through the mind of this man who seemed to be an introvert, a loner who opened to very few. But based on the intensity with which he prayed for the boy, we may be justified in thinking there may be a deep familial bond of some sort that God had allowed to grow.

In this life, God gives us many blessings and relationships are among the very dearest. Some we can, without great difficulty, say goodbye to once the season of that blessing is done. But some blessings—particularly relational ones—can be especially difficult to let go of. There may be something or someone in your life that appears to be uneclipsable and impossible to move on from. Yet, this may be precisely what God is calling you to do.

Some relationships we may keep for the whole course of our lives. It is possible if God allows it and both people are willing to put in the sacrifice and effort. The friend you meet for beer or coffee now in your 20s could be a friend that you still talk with in your 80s. It happens. But most blessings are only temporary. We may lose them due to natural causes or human sin. Other times we may be called to lay them down for the sake of Christ. If so, we will have to say goodbye to that blessing before we can embrace what God has for us next.

Saying goodbye to relationships that hold our affections is among the most difficult of challenges for God's men to face. There is a world coming where we won't have to say goodbye ever again. But this is not that world. In this world, many of our blessings fade. The Lord leads us to one and then to another. If we are to enter a new room, we must exit the old. When we fail to say goodbye, the blessings we try to hold on to may rot in our hands.

If God's men are to see reformation and revival in their generation, it will always be at personal cost. There will always be something we must leave behind. But if we sow it into eternity's soil, we will one day reap it in a far greater glory.

Prophets or Ideologues?

'Ahab called on Obadiah, a devoted follower of Yahweh.' -1Kg 18

Elijah first encounters Obadiah after he re-enters Israel. This isn't the Obadiah who wrote the short book bearing that name in the Old Testament. But this Obadiah is also a righteous bloke and it's important that we get our heads around his role within our story lest we have too narrow a view of what it means to be a witness for Christ in an apostate generation. If Elijah stands outside the system, confronts it, and seeks to persuade it to repent, then Obadiah is the spy working on the inside. He is working for the monarchy. But God uses him there and he is able to divert some household funds to a group of preachers in hiding at significant personal risk.

We have already looked at the subject of Elijah and misogyny. But we now need to draw another important distinction that is essential for our own souls. We need to recognise that's there is a difference between being a follower of the prophets and a mere confrontational.

I recently spoke with a friend of mine who works for a charitable organisation that on paper has 'a Christian ethos' but that has also foolishly hired some people who hold to some rather unbiblical ideas. He is a minority in his department, holding to Biblical convictions on evangelism, the gospel, gender, marriage, etc. He is in Obadiah's position—a godly man surrounded by people with ungodly heart.

In such situations, there is more than one way to go wrong. The first way he could drop the ball is the theme of much of this book—he could retreat in fear. He could be a coward and let the anxiety of the situation overwhelm him. Many men are cowards when they see God's truth being attacked. They remain silent in the face of intimidating ideologies that tell him to shut up.

But there is another pit we can fall in. We are called to turn *'neither to the left nor to the right'*. And if capitulating unthinkingly to 21st-century ideologies is turning to the left, then being a confrontational ideologue is turning to the right. By this, we mean a man who takes satisfaction in merely holding to right ideas. He looks down on those drowning in the insanity of our day and makes the same error as the Pharisee of old who prayed, '*I thank you God that I am not like that person.*' This man may be orthodox*, after a fashion, but he forgets the gospel. The corpse looks great, but it lacks a heart to make it alive.

In some ways, Obadiah is reminiscent of the prophet Daniel. Both worked behind enemy lines. If either of these men had gone around with a spirit of pride or being argumentative to their co-workers and bosses on a daily basis, they wouldn't have lasted very long. When it was time to speak the truth, Daniel spoke it. But otherwise, he was considerate to the pagans he worked with. A son of the prophets will be kind his neighbours regardless of what blasphemous creeds they hold. Yes, the church must debate. We must bring our ideas to the table. May we speak publicly, boldly, clearly and persuasively! But our goal is to save, not just to win. We seek to bring life. A man who is merely an ideologue will often be cantankerous and ungracious. If not motivated by grace, a man may use the excuse of 'speaking the truth' as a cover for mere belligerence. His goal is either to offend someone he's angry at or to simply win a debate. This sort of ideologue is often fighting against flesh and blood and argues far more than he prays. Though this man may make a lot of noise, the devil has little to fear from him.

---

* When we use 'orthodox' or 'orthodoxy' in this book, we are broadly referring to those matters that nearly all Christian teachers down through the centuries, the world over, have consistently affirmed until a very short time ago. If with a capital 'O' then we are referring to that formal branch of Christian profession, often called 'Eastern Orthodox'.

Don't focus on Jezebel

'Today I will reveal myself to Ahab.' -1Kg 18

Jezebel is the first Israeli priestess. Women were active and respected among God's ancient people. The roles of women as mother and homebuilder (Pr 14.1) were celebrated and honoured to levels far exceeding how they are viewed today. But though homeward roles were the norm, a woman's activity was not strictly limited to that. The Bible also records women being involved in business (Pr 31.16), contributing to Scripture (1Sam 2), military assassinations (Jd 4.21), and prophesying (2Kg 22.14). But in spite of this width of female flourishing, the role of the priest was one reserved for qualified men from the tribe of Levi.

This was not because a priestess is something unimaginable in the Ancient Near East—an era that many feminised moderns consider barbarically patriarchal. No. Israel is unique for *not* having a priestess. Jezebel, like Elijah's housemate, is Phoenician. It is Phoenician practice for a royal woman to be head priestess over Asherah, the deified morning star. Having a priestess involved in leading worship is normal in Phoenicia and among the other nations. So is the practice of addressing divinity as 'Mother'.

But Israel is different—or should be. She has a different theology and spirituality. And a different sexuality and understanding of gender flow from them. Israel is supposed to be a light. She is supposed to change the culture around her. But now darkness is invading the land.

Under Jezebel's influence, the people are now worshipping both a male and female deity and engaging in sexual behaviour that is condemned under God's Law. We might easily assume that Elijah will now confront Jezebel since she is the one really driving the new spiritual and sexual ideas of the day. We might, but we'd be wrong.

Though Elijah condemns Jezebel's teaching and practice, he doesn't focus on her. He focuses on the one to whom God gave the final authority: her husband, the King. The condition of the Kingdom is ultimately his responsibility. If Jezebel leads the people into sin, it is only because Ahab allows it. Elijah's call is not so much to push down Jezebel as it is to pull up Ahab—to be the King God desires him to be. Though Eve sinned first, and led her husband into the act of eating the fruit, Adam is condemned above Eve. He let it all happen. In Hebrew, the curse assigned to him is twice as long as the curse laid upon Eve. In Romans it is clear, '*Sin entered the world through one **man**.'*

A true Elijah ministry is never misogynistic even if some label it as such. Elijahian ministry doesn't focus on attacking godless women. It strives to raise up godly men who will raise up a godly nation. We might be tempted to excuse Ahab, saying he is simply a beta-male or has a laid-back personality. But Elijah confronts and condemns Ahab as the main cause of Israel's trouble. Israel is falling into abominable heresy and sin under his watch. Ahab abuses his authority by not using it and yielding it to the influence of his wife.

Elijah now calls his King and nation to 1,800 feet about sea level. He's going to confront all the blasphemy bishops of Baal and Asherah in a mighty showdown before everyone. He's believing for a demonstration of supernatural glory that hasn't been seen by God's people for centuries.

He's playing go big or go home.

The tension is building. But this scene isn't just something that happened long ago. It's happening now. We see Ahab everywhere today. Ours is a Mt. Carmel culture. Many homes and churches are falling into apostasy and, though godless women will be held to account for their own sin, the big failures of our day must ultimately be laid at the door of the spiritually sleepy Ahabs.

*

I was born to fight devils and factions. It is my business to remove obstacles, to cut down thorns, to fill up quagmires and to open and make straight paths.

If I must have some failing let me rather speak the truth with too great sincerity than once to act the hypocrite and conceal the truth.

-Martin Luther, c. 1517

#ElijahMen

The Lost Art of Truth-Telling

'I have not caused Israel trouble. You and your dad have.' -1Kg 18

Elijah steps once again before Ahab. It has been three years since their last date. During that time, Elijah has grown stronger in faith while Ahab has only grown in desperation to find the man whose word devastated the Israeli economy.

Ahab hates Elijah, but this loathing is not reciprocated. Elijah loves Ahab. Really. Ahab is his earthly King. He is the man he prays for and tries to turn back to God. But for real repentance to happen, strong words need to be said and received. This is not easy. Ahab has been led to believe—with Jezebel's help—that the nation's real troublemaker is Elijah. Before God's grace will move like fresh rain across the nation, Ahab must accept that the problems are rooted in his own rebellion against God. Ahab must come to see this and Israel must see it with him.

Our culture is terrible at truth-telling. We elevate the priority of being polite above the priority of being honest. We are godlessly nice. Christians are particularly terrible—so many of us run from proper, open debate. We have somehow come to define *love* as saying and doing only those things that leave our 'happy' emotions in a state of pure Zen. Sadly, social media trolls may be our best truth tellers. It is sad because trolls don't always tell the truth from hearts of mercy. There are very few 'trolls for Jesus' that are driven by kindness. And while it may be better to hear the truth from an uncharitable critic than not to hear it at all, it is not how God speaks. He speaks truth to save, not to condemn.

We often label truth tellers as 'rude' whether they are or not. But we need truth tellers because sin in us is constantly trying to suppress God's truth. We have no idea just how well we can lie to ourselves about the condition of our own soul. Really, we need a helicopter just to be able to properly survey the size of this ability. Self-deceit is something every human has a virtual Master's Degree in before we have learned to count.

Media and those around us reinforce these lies through conversations, books, social media, films, etc. Sometimes it even comes from a pulpit. That's why we need an army of truth-tellers to preach, write blogs, and (perhaps most effectively) to have sober conversations with those God brings into their lives.

As with Elijah, there will be times your truth-telling is rejected and labelled as hate speech.* Unfortunately, rejection by those we lovingly speak the truth to can begin to cultivate hatred in us. Don't let accusations of hate birth hate. Sin can be bitterly ironic like that. Don't let it. The best way to keep your heart right before God is to pray before you speak. Pray blessings on those you speak hard truths to. Weep over them in prayer long before you whip them with words.

We have already discussed the difference between a hate preacher and a prophetic voice. Hate preachers mostly operate within the church. Trolls† mostly operate in the world and mostly through electronic media. Hate preachers wear religious garb, but trolls tend to wear the garb of social or political expertise.

Trolls and prophets both speak painful truths. But trolls do it to win arguments. Prophets do it to win people. Trolls speak to get attention for themselves. Prophets speak to get glory for God. Trolls are always seeking to tear down. Prophets only tear down in order to build up. Trolls thrive on taking people into controversy. Prophets will take people through the controversy of hard truths, but only in order to get into the peaceful plane of righteousness afterwards.

And it is on this tall mountain near Israel's northern border with Phoenicia that Elijah seeks to take his people through the controversy and into the peace of Yahweh. He will be bold, sarcastic, and full on savage with the Monarch's monstrous messengers. They are, after all, more than just lost people. They are teachers and leaders who actively corrupt God's people. At such times, it is appropriate for holy men to speak God's truth in ways that are neither subtle nor moderate. Satan wants the church to shut up. He

---

* We should ask whether there even is such a thing as 'hate speech' in the sense that many today mean. Yes, we may use the term 'hate speech' when referring to words spoken in genuine hatred of another person. But its current cultural usage is far sloppier.

† Yes, there are some holy trollers out there trying to do good work, but this is not the majority of media trolls nor what most people think of when they hear the term.

doesn't want her to preach boldly. For if we stay silent or fail to show up to the debate, we lose.

The view over the Mediterranean is usually clear from Carmel. But there is a spiritual fog as thick as peanut butter on the land. A clear message spoken from a heart of love and confirmed by the power of the Holy Spirit is what's needed to face the fake prophets, cut through the pagan atmosphere, and persuade God's people to return. It's time to bring it like a boss.

The popular gospel of this day is the laughing-stock of Hell; it dares neither damn the sinner nor sanctify the saint.

-Catherine Booth

#ElijahMen

Elijah and the Lullaby Preachers

'How long will you waver between the two? If Baal is God, serve him. If Yahweh is God, serve him.' -1Kg 18

We have the summary of Elijah's sermon on Mt. Carmel. Like all good sermons should, it had just one point: *stop worshipping idols and start living for God.*

We don't know how long the sermon was. But I'm willing to bet that no one fell asleep. No one left Carmel that day thinking that Elijah had preached too long. Elijah's sermon and accompanying miracle so moved the people that they arose and killed the 450 false prophets of Baal as a response. It was effective. Granted, decapitating false teachers isn't exactly how we like to do things in New Testament times. But we shouldn't miss the obvious. People were stirred to do something dramatic upon hearing this message. True repentance happened that resulted in true action.

The Western church is now plagued with boring or powerless preaching. Not everywhere. But it's terrifyingly normal. Sadly, the most exciting sermons (in terms of delivery, not content) are often by blasphemers and fake teachers. It's tragic that on Sunday some may have to choose between a preacher who makes lies seem true or one who makes truth seem dull. Which is worse: the slick but sickening heresy peddled by religious salesman, or the garbled and mumbled impotence that is served up as a homily in old and dying churches? Even churches that are theologically solid too often seem to effectively communicate only to the 60+ age range. For too long theological institutions have bestowed upon the church orthodox yet docile clergymen. In such places, there is little fire in the pews because there is no furnace in the pulpit.

There was once a preacher in London that had a friend who was a successful actor. This actor packed out the theatres night after night. One evening over dinner, the preacher quipped to his friend, *'I would like to be able to fill my pews the way you fill your seats.'* The actor responded, *'The difference between myself and you preachers is that I take things that are unreal and*

50

make them seem real. You preachers take things that are real and make them seem unreal.'

Preacher, does your preaching sound like mere academic lectures or sentimental homilies? Is the goal of your message only to give information or bestow warm fuzzies? Or, are you preaching to give hell a headache and usher people into the presence of a holy God so they can repent and believe the Gospel? Do we know what Paul meant when he wrote, *'My preaching wasn't in word only, but in the power of God'*?

We don't mean hype. We don't mean eloquence, professionalism, or even being funny. We mean preaching with a conviction that shows your listeners you mean the things you say and are concerned for their eternal state. Many of us here in the UK preach as if we are going to be marked by professors for theological soundness at the end of our sermon. We rarely preach as dying men to dying men.

Our job is not to read sermon notes to our listeners or to just give them Bible trivia or homiletical balderdash. Our goal is to tell them about how the God of Scripture must change their lives through Jesus—or else. Remember, Jezebel's 850 fake teachers? They prophesied lies with a hellish passion. Our people face similar lies every week. We are to look people in the eye, confront society's lies, and try to soberly persuade them about who God really is and who they really are. We are to plead with them to repent and believe.

I sometimes hear older, orthodox ministers remark *'We are too old. We don't know how to speak to the younger generation.'* Dear fathers, please don't underestimate all you can do. We're not asking you to be very funny or learn all the modern slang. When this author was a teenager, it was an old preacher in his 80s that stirred him to a life of prayer. He was a man who desired revival more than his very life. There's a lot of young Skywalkers out there in need of an Obi-Wan. Don't belittle what God can do with man of any age that is possessed with His Spirit.

Church members, deacons, elders: when looking for a new minister, please let it be known that you are looking for more than a program director or ministry CEO. Make sure he knows that his top priority is to be prepared to speak with conviction on Sunday morning. Your pastor needs your open encouragement to spend those hours on his knees praying through the passage he will be expounding. The devil works to steal your pastor's time away from prayerful preparation with distractions. Help him to keep it.

Being faithful involves being more than stepping into the pulpit with orthodox sermon notes (if you use them). Being faithful also means preaching in the power of the Ghost. And that's not something you can get from a book. Fire for preaching comes from sucking the floor in your prayer closet. The great Scottish reformer, John Knox, used to pray, 'Give me Scotland or I die.' If we are willing to embrace that place in prayer, we open ourselves up to speak with a power that can transcend generational boundaries.

If we haven't prayed over the people and the passage, it will show when we open our mouths on Sunday. There is a generation of mischievous, orthodox young people that will give the devil hell—if only they are awakened and equipped. They need raven-preachers to bring them meat so they can grow.

Fake Prophets: Atheism

'Ahab gathered the prophets at Mt. Carmel.' -1Kg 18

Mt. Carmel is where Yahweh's sanctified spokesman confronts Jezebel's serpentine synod. The tension is similar to that of an old Western film. The cowboy walks back into town knowing that he is outnumbered. One Elijah confronts 850 foul friars of fake faith. But, as we will see, God's power is attracted to such weakness.

Many Christians today speak about the need to engage with culture. Yes, we do. But what many mean by this is that we need to compromise with culture, surrender to culture, or brown nose culture in hopes that the cool kids will think we are one of them.

Our prophet does none of those things. He knows that he faces an aggressive zeitgeist within the culture which demands that its own values to be celebrated. It is the same in all such times. But Elijah successfully engages them in truth and in the power of the Spirit while the demon-priests put on a show that we might find somewhere north of perverse. But in the debauched circus of crazed ideology, Elijah never encounters anything as singularly strange as Atheism. That odd spirituality won't arrive till a later generation.

Atheism is different to the other fake prophets we address here because it is not a significant influence within the church. I've only ever met a few people who identify as 'atheist-Christians'—and even they laugh about it. But though this isn't a significant corruption in the church, it is an active influence in the culture we are trying to reach.

There are many ways one may try to help an Atheist depending upon the relationship. Sometimes, a long-term relationship based on loving acts of kindness is what God will use to slowly melt an unbelieving heart. Other times it may involve God answering a prayer in a visibly miraculous way. Still other times, God might use a relationship based on a dialogue or debate. Here is a letter from an exchange I had with a former pastor who had backslidden into Atheism—a man that I have known for some years.

Since his 'deconversion', he often criticises bits of the Bible as being immoral. But if all human life consists of is energy and matter in motion, then where can we possibly get solid notions of what is moral or immoral? In a previous letter he tried to explain how a sense of altruism or morality might be the result of evolution. This is my response to that idea.

My Dear Atheist,

You wrote me to explain why you think it is no longer necessary to believe in God. I appreciate that. It was a friendly gesture. I hope you don't mind if I return my own thoughts - especially in response to what you wrote on morality and ethics. You say, 'Altruism is an evolutionary response to the pressures of competition in the world—we can't help but find it enjoyable.' So, according to your theory, we act in a moral way because evolution has designed us to get pleasure from doing so. We do good because it feels good. Is that it? Please let me briefly share four issues I have with your theory.

First of all, when some animals, our 'evolutionary cousins', eat their own children or when a male animal forces sex on a female, is this morally wrong? Can animals act in an immoral way? In your letter, you argue for 'a universal measuring stick'. But given the evolutionary process, how? Was there a definite moment in history when cannibalism and rape became wrong? If so, what year was it? Was rape ok for Neanderthals to do? If it's ok for some animals—and they seem to enjoy it—when did it become wrong for us?

Secondly, if morality evolves, what does this mean for other humans who do not share our moral standards? What about the barbarian Ghengis Khan and his crew? Did they act the way they did because they lived 900 years ago and evolution had not yet advanced their altruism to our level? Are we morally superior because 900 years has biologically advanced us? What about terrorists, Nazis, or ISIS? Does their behaviour show that they are genetically inferior to us? If our species is to advance, should we get rid of these altruistic retards? But then, if morality comes from our evolution, why berate immoral people? Why do you give, as you did in your letter, the ancient Israelis such a hard time? They were just doing what genetically gave them pleasure. You might as well call salmon to repent for not having legs.

Third, if altruism has developed to where it is now to help our species survive, should we expect it to change in the future? It's something always in motion that exists for the sole benefit of the survival of our species. Right? What if our hard wiring changes so that we see evil what we now see as good and vice versa? What if we start getting pleasure from other sorts of behaviours? Birth rates in the West are low. Perhaps our hardwiring will change in order to increase our offspring. It may have us do things to our women (rape?) that we now consider unethical so that they will have more babies. What if ISIS and their sex slavery, instead of being backwards, is really the next step in the evolutionary process to help replenish the species and make a stronger race? Perhaps evolution has noticed that not all humans are reproducing enough and put it into their heads to see sex slavery as good so that we might advance.

All that I'm saying here is consistent with your theory, right?

If morality evolved, then that means morality changes. Your eternal standard - which you say evolution can provide - is a concept foreign to the material universe you live in. The current morals of homo-sapiens are just a stopover on the road to something else. No use in getting too attached to them. Right?

Lastly, why should I be moral? You say it's because it gives me pleasure. Really? I'm sure I could find many things pleasurable that we would generally consider to be immoral. Couldn't you? In a given situation, why should I obey my altruism impulse, which you say that evolution gave me, but not obey my impulse for sexual satisfaction, for power, or for revenge? Did Evolution not give me those impulses too? Why is it wrong to follow the one impulse but not the other?

It is said that to a man with only a hammer, every problem is a nail. Could the same be said of many today in regards to science? That every issue can somehow be fixed by test tubes or understood by evolutionary theory? In your attempt to squeeze morality into the evolution box, it seems you have done great injustice to what we experience morality to be.

I leave it with you to respond.

Your friend,

-Joshua

Fake Prophets: Islam

'If Yahweh is God, follow Him. If Baal is God, follow Him.' -1Kg 18

I took some time to better familiarise myself with Islamic teaching when I was nineteen. I remember when I first read that Muslim men receive a paradise of seventy-two virgins as a reward if they die for their cause. At the time, I could understand the attraction. It seemed quite the Scooby Snack. Now that I'm a few years older and married with four children, the idea of having to teach seventy-two women how to have sex just seems like a lot of work.

Four or five maybe. But seventy-two?

A man has to know his limits.

Elijah confronts a plurality of beliefs on the mountain. Likewise, in our multi-kulti world, we also encounter a large buffet of ideas and one of the most popular dishes on the buffet at the moment is indeed Islam. Sadly, there are some teachers trying to mix the Gospel with this Mohammedan heresy under the banner of 'Chrislam'. (Really, it's a thing. Google it.) The condemnation of such teachers is just.

In recent years, there has been an increase in violence carried out by some who act in the name of Islam. Usually, there is shock and fear followed by people trying to calm the situation by reminding the public that most Muslims in the UK are moderate and not violent. And we understand the desire to do this. We can happily acknowledge that most Muslims are driven more by a desire to provide bread for their families than to destroy the infidels. Of course, some resent this endlessly repeated refrain and see it as politically correct jellyfishing. Some nationalists use such situations to lambast the whole Muslim community and we should resist such broad brushing.

Let's understand our priorities as Christians. It is understandable that secular people fear radical Islam. For those of us whose life is hidden with Christ in eternity, such fear is unnecessary though we still may feel it at times. Terrorism can make death more unpredictable and it may take our loved ones at unexpected times. But the ultimate tragedy of humanity is not that we lose loved ones when we least expect it—it's that we lose them in the first place. The goodbye we must one day make to all our loved ones is inevitable.

It's debated between radical and moderate Muslims to what degree the Qur'an encourages violence towards non-Muslims. This is because some verses are peaceful and some are violent in nature. But unlike the Bible, narrative context is not always clearly given to verses so it can be debated which ones are applicable in which situations. Some think Mohammed's later verses abrogate his earlier ones. But even this is not universally agreed upon.

What is certain is that the Qur'an denies Jesus' atoning death on the cross (Q4.157, '*They did not kill him nor did they crucify him.*') and it denies the hope of Christ's resurrection. Islam teaches that Jesus (Isa) was a mere prophet. This is why we must give ourselves to proclaiming the resurrection of Christ with fresh boldness and compassion. It is Christ alone that can save. If you have him, you no longer wet yourself at the thought of being murdered by a terrorist.

We should be concerned about the veils of both secularism and Islam. They both blind the people around us. The disease of sin is killing them and neither can cure. For this reason, I am more troubled by Islamic theology than by Islamic terrorism. Islam preaches a different Jesus. This Jesus did not die for sins, did not rise, and does not bring us into God's family. Islam does not teach that we need new hearts or that we can be born again. It teaches that we must simply choose to submit to Allah and hope on judgement day he has mercy on us. Iniquity is not a sickness in Islam, and there is, therefore, no need for a remedy.

We present Muslims with the Good News. A Messiah has come. He is the only one who has perfectly submitted to the will of 'Allah' and fulfilled all the commands—and he did it on our behalf. Jesus offers Muslims grace.

As a Christian, you have what they need.

Islamic theology is far more dangerous than a few explosions or knives. And so is any ideology, secular or religious, that blinds people from the person and work of Jesus. Yes, the bombs can be troublesome. But any theology that denies the death and resurrection of Jesus must be of far greater concern and it must be confronted.

Fake Prophets: Nationalism

'Elijah approached. "How long will you waver between two opinions?"' -1Kg 18

We need to speak about another fake prophet: race based Nationalism. Now both 'the Alt-Right' and 'Nationalism' are terms that have shades of meaning. Their usage varies a bit on both sides of the Atlantic. Yes, I know some non-racist people who self-identify as 'Alt-Right' to imply freedom of speech or Libertarianism. But the term is also used by many in the more specific sense of racial segregation or even white supremacy. Yes, it's true that all nations and races can be tempted to see their culture as the best. But we're talking about the Western church, so we'll focus primarily on Caucasian racism. This is a short reading, so please consider the context if I'm using terms a little differently than how you're used to.

Elijah loves his nation. He prays for Israel. But he is not a nationalist in the way most now use that term. There were many patriots who loved Israel as a nation who did not love Elijah. Likewise, Jesus himself was almost killed by the nationalists of his day for pointing out that Elijah went to care for a foreign woman during the famine and passed over the widows of Israel in doing so. Those patriots tried to throw him off a cliff for that observation.

As we speak openly about the dangers of Islamic theology, it could be easy to get swept up into the currents of a different demon. 21st Century European nationalism is a reaction to—among other things—poorly planned immigration policies and changes in culture by an influx of new arrivals who are not always assimilating well. Some of those here in Europe, who see the Islamic Crescent as a threat, have picked up the weapon of right-wing nationalism. In doing so they fight flesh and blood instead of spiritual powers. This patriotic swagger is not our calling. It is easier to fight *against* Muslims than it is to fight against Islam *for* Muslims. Our highest calling is to live for God's Kingdom and not simply to preserve Western culture.

This is not to slam European patriots or Western culture. My wife and I both enjoy and respect Western, classical culture and its great achievements. It is also understandable that many may want to preserve it and therefore limit outside influence. Sadly, this understandable desire to preserve the historical integrity of Western culture can often be misdirected as aggression at individual foreigners.

As Christians, we are not particularly interested in a wholesale protection of Western values. Yes, we appreciate what is good and beautiful. But not all Western values are Heaven's values. The same continent that gave us the beauty of Mozart also gave us the beast of Marxism. We appreciate what is good, but we do not romanticize our history. As Christians, we also know our final destination is a new heaven and a new earth. We are pilgrims. Countries like Switzerland, Sweden, Canada and the UK are temporary entities and excessive patriotism is a distraction from the real goal.

Ahab loves the nation of Israel more than he loves the God who raised up that nation. At the beginning of this chapter, Obadiah greets our prophet by saying, *'My lord Elijah'*. Ahab greets him with, *'You troubler of Israel'*. Why the difference in greeting? Both men hate the famine and its effects on the country. But Obadiah is aware of God's priorities and not just Israel's economy. Ahab was concerned about green grass. Obadiah was concerned about God's wrath.

Yes, it is ok to love European and Western culture. I do. It is ok to love the West's historic art, music, coffee, and food. I do too. But the Italian paintings of Michelangelo, the Austrian music of Mozart, the great Cathedrals, the American Bill of Rights, and the British Magna Carta will all one day turn to dust. It is human beings—from the well-off bank CEO in London to a refugee floating in an overcrowded raft in the Mediterranean—that lasts forever. It is them we must reach. We appreciate cultural treasures, but we have our marching orders. We are to make disciples of people from every tongue and tribe in every nation. We must keep the main thing the main thing.

European nationalists and the Alt-Right hate Islam. We as Christians should hate Islam too. But European Nationalists hate Islam for very different reasons. They hate Islam because it is changing European culture. Often, this hatred of Islam gets directed at the individual Muslims who are doing the changing on a grass-roots level. But the mission-minded Christian hates Islam precisely because he loves all people—Muslims and non-Muslims. And this makes all the difference. The Christian knows that Islam has blinded Muslims to the good news of forgiveness in Jesus. Though many of Europe's current immigration policies may have been poorly planned, churches with a gospel mindset will see this error as an opportunity to reach people for Christ they wouldn't have otherwise had a chance to share with.

The Alt-Right loves the Christendom of Europe more than it loves the Christ of Eternity. Its ultimate loyalty is not to Jesus. Race nationalism is only another path to paganism. Currently, the Alt-Right are portrayed in the news as being the antithesis of Antifa, cultural Marxists, same-sex marriage activists, and others that campaign on the social or political far left. Christians could easily buy into this superficial dichotomy between the far right and left, but we shouldn't. The differences only run but so deep. The signs held up at an LGBT parade may be different to the ones held up at an Alt-Right march, but ultimately, they are travelling in the same direction.

If Christ is not the Shepherd, then your tribe isn't headed to Heaven's pastures. It will either be the lust for political power and patriotism that leads your group, or it will be the lust for sex and self-identification. Without Jesus, either power or pleasure will be your culture's god. Some may dance to the beats of Sodom while others march to the rhythms of the Reich. But both bands are playing pagan poetry. Neither worship the Creator.

There is one road into Heaven. There are many roads into Hell—and by Hell, the racists have been fooled. They choose the Earthly kinship of race over and against the Heavenly kinship of Christ's church. They identify with those most like them in their first birth and so they forfeit the opportunity to have a second.

When calmly considered, a rational man may conclude that Islam is a threat to some Western values and treasures. There is nothing wrong with loving your European, British, or American neighbours by wanting to protect them from foolish political policies or campaigning for wise procedures of assimilation those to whom we do open our borders. This is wisdom. Christians may serve their home country in politics and sometimes loving your immediate neighbour might involve reforming immigration laws.

But wholesale political nationalism, racism, or a low view of foreigners only makes sense if you're a patriotic pagan. Not if you're a Christian. If you are a Christian who is particularly drawn to politics, be careful what you fight for. You are not called to fight against secularists, atheists, or Muslims. You are called to fight for those people—fight in prayer, love, hospitality, and in the humble sharing of who Jesus is.

Fake Prophets: JezebeLGBT

'The prophets of Asherah.' -1Kg18

The Elijah saga may—at first glance—seem to have nothing to do with gay sex. But if we take off our 21st Century cultural glasses and read with an Ancient Near Eastern view, that misconception soon vanishes.

The Bible uses the term *'sexual immorality'* like a junk drawer—all sorts of things get thrown in there. There are lists in places such as Leviticus 18 and 20 which spell out in detail what we put in it. *Animals?* Yep, put it in the drawer. *Is she my sister?* Yep, put that in the drawer too. *My Aunt? Another bloke?* Yep, put it all in the drawer. If it involves sex outside of the one man, one woman marital covenant, it almost certainly goes in that drawer.

The Bible also does not presume the sharp distinction between homosexual and heterosexual 'orientations' that we do today. And the Bible is not alone in that regard. The whole idea of 'orientations' is quite a new concept. In the ancient world of the Greeks and Romans, it was thought that most men would experiment in sexual activities of various sorts: wives, girlfriends, prostitutes, concubines, male lovers, boys, etc. Much of history has presumed a greater possible fluidity in terms of sexual desire than that which Western culture developed during the late 20th/early 21st Century. *Sure, some may have a general preference. But why limit yourself?*

In part, this tendency to see sexual desire as something that was immovably fixed came from the LGBT campaign strategy of comparing the gay rights cause to that of racial segregation. *'Gay is the new black!'* it was proclaimed. Though there was never any science to confirm this notion, it is still held to by many activists as it is thought to give moral force to their objectives. Stories that involve same-sex attracted individuals experiencing genuine change towards opposite sex attraction are often attacked or ridiculed as they seem to work against the 'fixed' narrative.

We say all that to help us understand our current place in history. Our rigid understanding of 'orientations' is new, but gay sex is not new. Culturally celebrated gay sex is not new. This is important because when we read about the sexcapades that accompanied the Asherah poles and other types of Baal and Canaanite worship in Elijah's day, we may just think of men knocking boots with female prostitutes. We would be wrong to do so. Canaanite sex was as rainbow parading as one could get and probably had even more letters than our current always growing LGBTQI alphabet.

So, when Jezebel came on the scene, it wasn't just hetero-sex* outside of marriage she was promoting. It was homo-sex as well. Israeli men would have been encouraged to experiment with both. As we will touch on in the next reading, this was also the case in Jesus' day. Those who say Jesus never spoke on gay sex should have a closer look on what 1st century Jews understood by the term 'sexual immoralities'.

LGBT ideology and practice is currently a huge social topic. Sadly, it is not just a phenomenon in society. These ideas and practices are infecting churches, even ones that think of themselves as 'Evangelical'. Many pastors who know better, stay silent from the pulpit as they fear a negative backlash. They say they don't address the issue publicly because *everybody knows where we stand*. But in reality, people in the church are very confused. These next three readings deal with homo-sex from a standpoint of cultural engagement. They are slightly longer than other readings.

Christians are not *obsessed with gay sex* as some have suggested. Nor do most Christians think that individuals who struggle with homosexual sins are worse than those who struggle with the common hetero damnables. We openly acknowledge that pornography, divorce, and hetero fornication in the church are all sins that are more frequently committed. Yes, we will deal with pornography and other transgressions relevant to straight blokes later. We—who struggle with typical heterosexual temptations—are no better than our brother who struggles with same-sex attraction. We stand arm-in-arm as comrades against the onslaughts of hell.

The reason we rightfully focus on this issue is that there are no Fornication Pride parades happening in my city that I know of. There are no

---

* I'll occasionally use the terms *hetero-sex* or *homo-sex* for the technical reason of wanting to clearly refer to specific acts instead of the terms *heterosexuality* or *homosexuality* which, depending on the context, can be more vague.

teachers of influence who creatively recontextualize and reread the Scriptures in order to justify pornography. Though the deeds themselves may be more frequently committed by professing believers, I don't know of any people who proudly identify themselves as 'adultery Christians' or 'porn-again Christians'. But I do see many who identify as 'gay Christians'—and they usually mean more by that term than simply having same-sex attraction.

Nor are churches being directly pressured by powerful political forces to change their views on doubt, polygamy, adultery, or drunkenness. But within the last year alone Speaker of the House John Bercow has advocated for the right of same-sex couples to get 'married' in any church they want. Presidential candidate Hilary Clinton made similar calls during her campaign in the USA. Such comments are frequently heard. We are not being asked to tolerate the ideology behind gay 'marriage'. We are being told that we must celebrate it.

There is also a huge amount of fake information at the moment on this subject. It is affecting how people read the Bible. Some are introducing previously unheard-of ways of interpreting Scripture in order to get around verses that have been understood to be quite clear on this issue for mileia.

The pressure is real. Things will get worse before they get better. You may think that you and your church are cool with the surrounding culture. Perhaps you are. Kudos. But there will soon come a time when many people will not care about your hip tattoos, how savvy you are with coffee and skinny jeans, or that you're well versed with all the latest bands. Some people will hate you simply for saying that sex is for one man and one woman in the context of one lifelong marriage. There's nothing wrong with being able to speak the language of culture. It is often comendable. But do not be naïve. Standing for righteousness will often cause you to be hated by the world no matter how humble or hip you might articulate it. You will be seen as a neo-Nazi for simply professing a righteous view of sexuality.

The battles surrounding homosexual activity and the way we engage it with Scripture are central to the reform of the church in our generation. Confronting this spiritual strongman within the church will take a combination of courage and compassion. Courage, in confronting the demonic ideology and its fake teachers. And compassion, with a listening ear, to those lost or those believers affected by it.

Dear Pro-Gay Christian

'The prophets of Asherah.' -1Kg 18

Elijah does not engage the prophets of Baal the way he did with the Phoenician widow. Yes, she worshipped the same idols they did. But one relationship was marked by gentle care while the other was characterised by bold confrontation. Likewise, there is a world of difference in how one approaches the homosexuality issue depending on the circumstances. If you are reaching out in care to the unbelieving, lesbian couple next door, that requires humility, grace, and a servant's heart. If we are counselling a 15-year-old boy in our youth group who is opening up for the first time about his same-sex desires, that requires compassion and a listening ear.

But if you are facing the Rainbow Blitzkrieg as it ploughs its way through the church with its propaganda pieces, activists and the media spotlight gets put on you, well, that is quite a different matter. When you get put on the spot and others are looking to see if you will bow the knee to Queen JezebeLGBT and spout the culturally accepted view on the issues, then a backbone of steel and words of fire are what is needed. We address those who struggle with doubts with a gentle vocabulary. But with those who promote sin and fake teaching in the church, we are not to mince words.

Here is an example. A letter posted on a blog went viral. You can still find it online. In it, a fake teacher rejects an orthodox Christian as a friend. She does so because she thinks—given this Christian's views—he only wants to hang out with her in order to be seen as culturally savvy. She presumes that, if an orthodox Christian really does see gay sex as a sin, the only reason such a one would want to reach out in friendship is simply for the social capital of being able to say, *'I have a gay friend.'* The letter stirred my Protestant soul and my fingers started protesting on the keyboard. She addressed her letter to a *'Non-affirming Christian'*. Here is my letter in response...

Dear Pro-Gay Christian Friend,
Thank you for taking the time to write me. Sadly, it seems you misunderstand

why I met with you for coffee. Please let me explain my motives by defining the words in my salutation above. Would this be too terrible a way to go about it?

Let's start with *'friend'* shall we? You rightly question this term as an accurate description of our relationship. For now, let's simply say I mean it as an expression of goodwill. But we will return to it again at the end of the letter.

Then there's this term, *'pro-gay'*. By this, I don't mean your personal sexual urges. There have historically been—and are today—countless godly leaders in the church who have deep sexual and romantic attractions to people of the same gender. In spite of their desires, they remain celibate and teach orthodox views of gender and marriage. In your letter, you repeatedly refer to me as a *'non-affirming Christian'*, but I affirm these people and what they teach.

What I do mean by *'pro-gay'* is the teaching you now promote through personal conversations and social media. The articles you share, the comments you leave, and the blogs you write all teach that active sex between two people of the same gender is acceptable to the God of the Bible. It's not that you are merely wrestling with questions. You promote a particularly Western, 21st Century view of sexuality that is counter to what God's people have historically believed and faithfully taught for millennia by affirming sexual activity outside the orthodox understanding of marriage.

Now, this wouldn't be a problem if you were one of my non-Christian family members or friends that hold to this view. I see this teaching appear in memes and sound bites from them every day. But you do all this while naming Christ. That's different. Paul makes this distinction in 1 Cor 5,

> *'I have told you to avoid sexually immoral people, but I didn't mean the immoral of this world. You would have to leave the world for that! I mean anyone who calls themselves a believer and does so. Avoid them! I should only judge those in the church, not those outside the church.'*

And this is where we come to the third term in my salutation, *'Christian'*. How do you define this? I'm sure you are aware that for over 98% of Christian history the idea that our faith is in any way compatible with homosexual practice would've been unthinkable. *'Pro-Gay Christian'* would've seemed as outrageous a term as, *'pro-thievery Christian'* or *'pro-pornography Christian'*.

And this is why it is sad just how profoundly you misunderstood our coffee date. Your letter suggests that I met you to garner acceptance points with the cool kids. That's an unfortunate interpretation. Rather, I wanted to warn you that you're in risk of rejection from the only One whose opinion actually matters.

Not only did your letter contain many strawmen misrepresentations of what Christians actually believe but some of the articles you share on social media refer to Christians as *'homophobes'* and *'haters'* for simply believing what

Christians have almost always believed—that marriage is a sacramental covenant between a man and a woman. Even in your letter to me, you refer to this aspect of Christian faith as a *'murderer'*. I expect such hostile pejoratives and misrepresentations from the world around me. I don't expect that from someone who names Christ.

By being willing to *'hear your story'* (as you say in your letter) you imply that I was disingenuous and only wanted to use you for some insincere end, to gain social capital. No. I was trying to give you every possible chance to explain why you would be promoting an ideology that is an enemy to our faith. I was hoping against hope that you had somehow misunderstood the issue. But as you explained over your latte how you now see the Bible as a *'general guide and not as a strict rulebook'* it became clear that you understood the issues just fine.

In Revelation chapter two, Jesus speaks of a woman in Thyatira who is promoting an ideology of sexual immorality in his name. He gives her time to repent but, if she does not, he promises to remove her harshly. I care for you and don't want you to come under judgement. That's why I wanted to meet—to plead with you. But all I heard from you were the same lines I hear from my non-Christian friends every single day. I was looking at you as a person, but all I heard from your mouth was the spirit of this age.

You said that you cannot be my *'gay Christian friend'*. Sadly, I must now return the favour and say that I can't be your orthodox Christian friend. At least not 'friend' in the classical sense of the word. And it is not because of your sexual desires. If you had doubts, that would be fine. We could talk. If you were one of my unbelieving family member or friends that happen to be gay, there would be no problem. If you were same-sex attracted, that would be fine too. I would never reject you on the basis of something you can't control. But you are going public with fake teaching that promotes immorality and openly acting out in sinful, sexual behaviour. I must now obey Scripture and distance myself from you for the sake of those in the church that you are trying to influence.

But if you ever want to really talk again, if you want to reconsider your ways, the light is always on for you.

You repeatedly refer to me in your letter as *'non-affirming'*. I'll accept that label, but so must you. We are just non-affirming about different things. You won't affirm Christian sexual orthodoxy. I won't affirm your attempt to baptise buggery.

-Joshua

It is treason against the King of Kings to tone down the word of the Lord.

-CH Spurgeon

Is Jesus Silent on Homosexuality?

'I have not come to destroy the law.' -Matt 5

Many of us have personalities that don't enjoy debate. It's not that we are snowflakes who absolutely need safe space or we burst into tears. We simply don't enjoy arguing. And that's fine. But as there are those who, in the name of Christ, are saying that we need to adjust our teaching to the new LGBTQ ideology, then a debate is upon us whether we enjoy it or not. Some of us must do it and we must all be able to respond when asked.

In any discussion involving people's lives, points of view need to be expressed accurately—especially this one. Misinformation, however well intended, helps no one in the long run. That is why it is important to examine popular sound bites that are often used in social media discussions to determine whether they are based more on facts or feelings. One line used by those waging the current propaganda war upon us is: *Homosexual practice is consistent with Christianity because Jesus never spoke against it.* It is used enough for us to take a close look at his claim.

For those who are not Christians, this issue may stir mild curiosity. But for Christians, knowing what Jesus thought about any issue is of utmost importance. That is why it is right that we ask: *what does the evidence suggest about Jesus' thoughts on this subject?* Is Jesus totally silent on the issue like some say? Or, can we discern from the evidence that Jesus does have a view of human sexuality that has obvious implications for our gay sex and gay marriage discussions?

First of all, arguments from silence are rarely successful in accomplishing their goal, whatever the discussion may be. If my aim is to argue that some popular figure would endorse a lifestyle choice of mine just because they have never been on record as speaking against it, then I make myself vulnerable to all sorts of rebuttals. Whatever one's view in the current sexuality and gender debate may be, an argument from silence is never a strong one. Especially when it comes to things Jesus supposedly said or did not say. If we want to play this card, then we also must admit that Jesus never spoke directly about genocide or wife beating either. But the fact that he didn't specifically mention them by name does not give us license to assume he approves of them, much less that we should automatically participate in these activities.

But should we assume that Jesus was completely silent on this issue? Yes, many people say so—especially online. But is this statement true? Let's look at three passages from Matthew's gospel where Jesus seems to be making statements that are relevant to the issue, then decide for yourself.

Don't assume that I came to destroy the Law or the Prophets. I did not come to destroy but to fulfil. For I assure you: Until heaven and earth pass away, not the smallest letter or one stroke of a letter will pass from the law until all things are accomplished.
–Matt 5.16-18

Jesus upholds all previous prophets. It would be difficult for Jesus to say this any clearer. Whenever Moses and other prophets discussed the activity of gay sex (not merely attractions) it was always negative. Yes, Jesus fulfilled ceremonial law and cleanliness laws and, for that reason, we no longer do certain things like sacrifice animals. Those laws are not erased, just fulfilled in Christ who is our continual priest and sacrifice for sin. But all the moral law (lying, stealing, adultery, etc) and social principles (love your neighbour, care for the poor) are still there. Jesus warns us against disobeying these moral laws or teaching others that it's ok to do so.

But that is not the only relevant verse in Matthew. Jesus then says, '*For from the heart come evil thoughts, murders, adulteries, sexual immoralities, thefts, false testimonies, blasphemies. These are the things that defile a man.*' (Matt 15.19) Here, Jesus gives us a list of what defiles us. You see that fourth term in the list, '*sexual immoralities*'. Notice the plural. Does it seem strange? Why is that term plural? Why not just say that '*sexual immorality*' defiles a man?

There is a reason it is in the plural. The Greek word used here is *Porneia*—from where we get the word '*pornography*'. As we said earlier, this is a junk drawer term where we can put all sorts of sexual sins. But the Hebrew people were quite specific in what should be put in that drawer. For the people of God, Leviticus 18 and 20 were the *Porneia* laws list - and yes it included male-male sodomy. There would not have been a single Jew in Jesus' audience who would have thought that Jesus did not also imply homo-sex (along with all other sorts of hetero-sex sins) when he said *'sexual immoralities defile you'*.

Lastly, Jesus speaks about God's intention for human sexuality while debating divorce:

> *'Haven't you read,' He replied, 'that He who created them in the beginning made them male and female,' and He also said: 'For this reason, a man will leave his father and mother and be joined to his wife, and the two will become one flesh?' So they are no longer two, but one flesh. Therefore, what God has joined together, man must not separate*
>
> -Matt 19.4-6

In his debate with other religious leaders, Jesus quotes from the book of Genesis as an authoritative source—meaning that Jesus still thinks Moses is relevant and should be listened to. In doing so, Jesus affirms the gender binary and that the difference between the two genders is the basis for a marriage that should last a lifetime. Though Jesus' direct object of debate here was divorce, can we see the rather obvious implications for the current debate over gay 'marriage'? Is this passage really completely irrelevant?

Trinity
Finally, in saying that Jesus *'never said anything about homosexual practice'* one is implying that Jesus had nothing to do with the writings of Moses and the prophets before his earthly ministry. We are also saying Jesus had nothing to do with the writings of Paul and the other apostles after his earthly ministry—writings that deal very directly with homosexual practice.

As Christians, we cannot agree with this presumption. We believe that God is a triune God—the Father, Jesus the Son, and the Holy Spirit. We believe this one God inspired the writings of the Bible and was fully and equally involved in all of God's words and acts throughout it. So, when Moses wrote Leviticus, Jesus was there. When Paul wrote 1 Corinthians under divine inspiration, Jesus was there. And when God rained down fire on Sodom, Jesus was there—in full participation and full agreement.

The Wedding Invitation

We've seen Elijah befriend a woman from a culture that was spiritually and sexually pagan. Though she did ultimately come to have faith in Yahweh, it took some time to get there. Our sexuality flows from our spirituality, so giving advice about sex to someone who doesn't share your faith can be complicated. Ultimately such people don't need good advice, sexual or otherwise. Their deepest need is good news.

Here is another letter. It is different than the previous one. The last one was written to a professed Christian actively promoting LGBT ideology among other Christians. This letter is to a non-Christian friend. Note the difference in tone. Though this letter was never given to one specific person, it is not right to say it is fake. It is based on conversations I've had with non-Christian LGBT friends and family on this specific issue. It is more composite than fictitious.

> *Dear Katie,*
>
> I hope this letter finds you well. You've been on my mind lately as it's been a few weeks since we've met up. We're overdue to grab a coffee—I hope we can soon. I also want to thank you for thinking of me as you sent out invitations for what I know will be a big day for you and Joanna. I've known you since before you met her (two years ago now, is it?) and I appreciate all you've shared with me about how meaningful that relationship is to you.
>
> It was especially kind of you given my Christian faith. You've never directly asked me my views on gender or sex in much detail. But I think our conversations must have touched on it enough to at least make you a bit unsure of my reaction when you sent the invitation.
>
> I have to say 'no' to your kind invitation. You know that I care for you and that I value our friendship. You also know that I've never rejected you because of your desires or relationship with Joanna. Because of that, you may be wondering, or perhaps even confused, as to why I would turn it down. If you don't care to hear my thoughts, then please throw this letter away now. But if you are genuinely wondering 'why?', then please read on as I'd like to explain myself.

You know from all the discussions we've had that I respect your intelligence, so I trust you won't see the style of my writing as 'mansplaining', but rather as an attempt to write simply so that I don't wrongly express myself or my faith.

You have rarely talked to me about my faith and my few attempts to bring it up has not, seemingly, met with much interest on your end. You asked me once what God thought about cheap beer and 80's music. (He's not a fan in case you've forgotten). But our talks have revealed that we still share the love of many things: culture, films, music, books, and spiced rum.

But my relationship to God isn't just a small piece of my life that can fit neatly into a drawer. It's rather a pair of glasses that enables me to see and interpret everything else—just as your atheism affects everything you see—be it consciously or unconsciously. It's because we each wear different glasses that my declining to attend a day that is important to you may not make any initial sense.

Your atheism posits that all the world is the result of time and chance acting upon matter. But as a Christian, I believe the world was created with a purpose, to be received and experienced with gratitude, and lived out with the intention it was created for. For that reason, you see our mutually beloved spiced rum differently than I do. You see it through the materialistic lens. You see your taste buds as the fruit of evolved bacteria that just so happen to derive pleasure when put in contact fermented molasses.

You may give thanks to me if I happen to buy you the drink, but that's the extent of your gratitude. I see the rum differently. God knew we'd figure out how to make rum and so he gave us taste buds specifically to enjoy it. He also gave us cinnamon and other spices so that we could blend the rum in a way that angels approve of. God allowed us to discover rum because He is good, wants us to be happy, and give Him thanks. We both enjoy it. But for me, it's an act of worship. For you, it's a chance meeting of molecules. Our rum drinking is different because our universes are different.

The same is true for my sex. Like rum, we may both enjoy sex. But I have sex different from you. And that's not just because I'm a bloke. As an atheist, you see sex as one of the accidents of the universe—more pleasurable than most perhaps—but still purposeless in the ultimate sense of the term. But as a Christian, I believe sex is a gift given by a kind God whose heart is bigger than Christmas. It's a gift that is intensely purposeful and we should not use it in accordance with any impulse we may experience. Like electricity, sex is a great gift—but misuse of that powerful gift may harm. We have many rules regulating how electricity is managed in public places. We do this, not because we don't value our citizens, but because we do.

God knew that He was going to save the world through Jesus sacrificial death and that He would be with His people in full, unrestrained love forever. Because God knew that's where He was taking human history, He created male and female and established marriage as the life-long union of one man and one woman and that relationship is to be the one place where sexual activity is done.

He does this for everybody's sake (including those who are single) so that we can all see and be reminded of where God is taking history. The husband is to love his wife as Christ loved the church and the wife is to respect her husband as the church does Christ. Marriage and sex—when used in the way God created—give the world a picture of who God is.

You may be tempted to think that my ultimate desire for you is that you 'be straight'. No. In my neighbourhood, I am surrounded by married heterosexuals who have prospering mutual funds, but bankrupt souls. They don't know their Creator and their heterosexuality doesn't earn them any brownie points with Him. My desire for you is that you'll come to know this God. You may call this my (ahem) missionary position. And so it is. It's a position borne out of friendship. Though you express little interest in getting to know the One who has given you so much, you're still invited to His house and I hope you will.

You may also be tempted to think that I see your relationship with Joanna as being all evil. This is not the case either. There's much good that I see in your relationship. You love one another, care for one another, and enjoy each other's company. It seems you are good friends, and friendship is a gift from God.

My belief is that God has given us sex for a purpose and that using that gift for other purposes only causes harm in the long run. That's why I cannot celebrate this day with you—because I think there is something better. Of course, given your atheism, any talk of purpose (and therefore sin) is silly. Life has no ultimate purpose and therefore purpose cannot be misdirected.

I know some Christians who would acknowledge everything that I've written above about the Biblical purpose of sex, yet they would still attend the ceremony out of affection for you as their friend. I feel the weight of that. But the more I consider that the more convinced I am that it would be unloving to attend. Given my beliefs about the universe, humans, life, sex, and love, being there would only be hatred dressed in a suit of politeness. Do you really want me to celebrate something with you that I think will bring you harm in the long run? If there's one thing that we both share, it's that neither of us like fake people—and showing up would be polite fakery.

I understand if my refusal stings. Please consider it from my point of view. From my end, I would love to continue the friendship we've enjoyed over the last four years. Like rum and sex, I've received your company as God's gift.

Every kind intention,

-*Joshua*

The God of Patriarchs

'God of Abraham, Isaac, and Jacob, let it be known that you are God.' -1Kg 18
'They are loved because of the Patriarchs.' -Rom 11
'In the spirit of Elijah, he will turn the hearts of the fathers to their children.' -Luke 1

Elijah prays to the God of the three men known throughout Scripture and church history as *'the Patriarchs'*. He cries to the God of Abraham, Isaac, and Jacob. He publicly addresses Yahweh before the multitude in this fashion to contrast the spirituality and sexuality that he proclaims against that of Jezebel. He calls his generation to choose between two opposing ways of seeing the world. The difference between them affects everything from how we pray, to what we do with our pants, to what marriage means.

Patriarchy is currently a socially charged term and open discussion on the topic is often difficult as is any subject that is to do with gender or gender roles. The ASA here in Britain passed a law this year against the display of women in traditional roles in advertising. Theoretically, this means that a woman cannot be displayed in an advertisement picking up children's socks in the living room unless she is also displayed marching through the desert carrying a sledgehammer and wrestling an alligator.

Many Feminists take it as their war cry to *'smash the Patriarchy'*. But not only is *patriarchy* a term that triggers, it is a term filled with ambiguity and confusion. *Just what is it exactly that we are talking about?* This makes it even more difficult as the term evokes different ideas for different people. There is 19th Century Victorian Patriarchy, Islamic Patriarchy, Greco-Roman Patriarchy, and Biblical Patriarchy. Some believe that we should smash everything even connected with this term regardless of cultural or historical context. Others believe we need to look closer and be more nuanced in what we choose to reject, lest we throw out the father with the bathwater.

Patriarchy has not always been a charged term. Not long ago in Western culture, patriarchy was generally understood to mean the process that most young men went through in order to become men. For a man to be taken seriously, he had to demonstrate a capacity to work hard and wise enough to be able to support a wife and raise well-adjusted children. This understanding has not been completely lost. Even today, there are men who can testify that marriage andchildren has forced them to lovingly lead and sacrifice in ways that laziness and moodiness in them would not have wanted. Being challenged to do marriage and family in godly ways changes us and pushes us to lead in ways that our passive inner-Ahabs may naturally resist. Yes, some men choose not to marry and employ their talents in other fruitful ways—and we will talk about the gift of celibacy later. But celibacy is the exception, not the rule.

Though historically noble, *Patriarchy* has developed a new connotation over the last few decades, and it is not a good one. Whereas the understanding of the word used to focus on the responsibility of the maturing young man, it now implies the oppression of women. It has gone from something to be applauded to something to be abhorred. Most modern Feminists now want to smash everything under this banner of Patriarchy without taking the time to appreciate the vast differences that exist between the various systems associated with this term. This goes from the most ignorant Neanderthal that thinks that girls should not be able to read and rules his house like a dictator all the way to the soft and tender 'mild complementarian*' who always wears cardigans and is constantly apologizing to Feminists for how horrible men are. Modern feminists want to smash the whole thing. They want to smash all the various worldly patriarchies as well as Biblical patriarchy.

With Feminists, Christians should agree that there are some things called *Patriarchy* that should be smashed. We can agree that there is much oppression of women in this world and rightfully denounce it. Some MRA (Male Rights Activist) readers may be quick to add there are also ways that men are treated unfairly. Quite. We will address that later. For now, let us agree that the widow burnings of India, the acid attacks in the Middle East, the wife beating of North Africa, and female genital mutilation are all forms of female oppression that should be resisted by followers of Christ. If such acts are what people have in mind when the term *Patriarchy* is used then 'no', we should not be patriarchs. Give us a hammer, let's start smashing.

---

* If you're unfamiliar with the discussion between 'complementarians' and 'egalitarians' regarding gender in the church, take a moment to google these terms and familiarise yourself with them. We will touch on the subject again later in the book.

But these things are not what the Bible or Christians have historically meant by the term. Some mix this sort of violent oppression up with other things and soon ideas get muddled and we end up passing around ideological cocktails into the conversation. These cocktails are made by those who have an agenda that they want to sneak through instead of subjugating it to clear and open debate. This is sad. Because under the banner of *'smashing the patriarchy'*, we usually end up not addressing the areas of the world where women are oppressed the most. Instead, many use the expression to promote certain gender heresies here in the West. And the results have been unfortunate.

In pursuit of revival and reform, the Western church needs to rediscover what the Bible—not culture—means by patriarchy. Culture changes. We would label the Angles and the Saxons of the 5th-10th Century as patriarchal, yet they had much more open ideas about gender roles than the more narrowly defined ideas of the Normans who invaded our islands in 1066. Often those who reject Patriarchy outright have a particular idea in mind and fail to consider the good some forms of Patriarchy have brought the family unit and wider culture over the millennia in cultures around the world. Today in the UK we have over 3 million children going to bed each night without a father. They are not fatherless because of too much Patriarchy. They are fatherless because young men are not raised with a vision of manhood that involves marrying a woman and raising healthy, loved children. Instead, thanks to fifty years of social engineering that has been introduced under the banner of *liberation*, young men are raised to think that manhood involves drinking loads of alcohol and sleeping with as many girls as possible without having to accept responsibility for unwanted children. In the 21st Century, young women are often treated with all the respect of a used car and young men continue to act like boys well into their early 30s—if not longer. This would have met with much social shame 60 years ago. But today, few people care. Could our lack of young men interested in marriage and children be the fruit of indiscriminately *'smashing the Patriarchy'*?

God created sex, marriage, and children to be a one package deal. One man, one woman, one lifetime—that is the context for sex. If a young man wants sex, he needs to demonstrate first that he has what it takes to be a good husband and good father. Sex was not seen as a right. It was seen as a privilege—a privilege for a man who was mature, capable, and ready to take a wife. Separating these things has done far more harm to women in the West than all the individual cases of hyper-patriarchal abuse combined. Sadly, it is often Feminist groups that promote these notions, thus betraying the women they claim to work for.

Yes, there will be some men who will choose to forgo marriage to better serve God. Elijah was one. But most will serve God in marriage and by being fruitful and multiplying. Raising young men with a vision to marry and raise up children flies counter to the laddish culture of today. Our culture does not raise a lot of men. It raises a lot of ageing boys.

Some of what is written here may be triggering. And, granted, a word of warning is in order. While we need to affirm the Creational gender binary and celebrate the uniqueness that exists between men and women, we must do so while holding up an obligatory caveat as many Christians tend to swing from one extreme to another. When some speak about rediscovering the godly development of boys into men, traditional ideas are often imported. We need to be careful here. We should not assume that everything done in the past was good, nor that all Feminist achievements are essentially bad. As we've said, some things that are called *Patriarchy* should be smashed. I have several books on my shelf written by women. I have learned a great deal from these ladies. I find the writings of Amy Carmichael and Catherine Booth to be particularly full of fire.

A barracks is meant to be a place where real soldiers were to be fed and equipped for war, not a place to settle down in or as a comfortable snuggery in which to enjoy ourselves. I hope that if ever they, our soldiers, do settle down God will burn their barracks over their heads!

-Catherine Booth
Speaking about her hopes for the future of the
Salvation Army which she and her husband William started.

It would be easy to embrace ideas of faux manhood or womanhood from traditional culture instead of from careful exegesis of the Bible. It could also be easy to create legalisms and become gender Pharisees. Culture varies and there is freedom in the methods we might use in the raising of men (so long as our goal is just that: raising men). We are not trying to establish *Pride and Prejudice.*

Nor do we want the sort of Patriarchy described in the Qur'an*. Simply reacting to laddish culture without careful Biblical reflection can create stifling gender roles that oppress instead of ones that direct and cultivate actual maturity. We are called to follow Christ, not the Sultan or Mr Darcy.

Confronting a laddish culture that seeks sex without children is an Elijah ministry. The angel Gabriel declared about John the Baptizer that he would be like Elijah in turning *the hearts of the fathers back to the children*. This is what the Bible means when it speaks about Patriarchy: men whose hearts are set on children. Abraham was a Patriarch because of his heart for Isaac and his desire raise up decedents that would serve Yahweh.

Men: if you get married and seek to do this in a God-honoring way, you will suffer. To righteously lead one of God's daughters and her children will involve the regular sacrifice of your own dreams and desires. It means getting off your phone and playing with your children. It means talking with and listening to your wife when you would prefer a nap. Anyone who thinks Biblical Patriarchy means the bloke gets to do whatever he wants has not done his homework and is still ignorant of what Christ-like leadership means. You are a heretic and not orthodox in your Patriarchy. Being a Biblical Patriarch means having a vision of seeing your grandchildren preach the gospel and worship Jesus—and having this vision 25 years before they are even born. A Biblical Patriarch is one who prays for his descendants to honour and obey God, long before he even has any.

A Biblical Patriarch lays down his life for his family. And it is to the ultimate Patriarch who will one day make this ultimate sacrifice that Elijah now prays.

---

* See Surah (chapter) 4.34-35 of the Qur'an. Sayyid Abul Ala Maududi (the preeminent Islamic commentator of the 20th Century) writes of this verse in his internationally read tafsir (commentary), 'Qawam *stands for a person who is responsible for the right conduct, safeguard and maintenance of the affairs of an individual, an institution or an organization. Thus, man is governor, director, protector and manager of the affairs of women.*'

The Gospel According to Elijah

'Elijah prayed, "Hear me, Lord, so that these people may know that you are God and that you are turning their hearts back to you."' -1Kg 18

Elijah seems to stand alone at the serpentine synod. But a man who walks with God is never alone. He beings to pray before the King, the crowd, and the counterfeit clergy. His prayer reflects the eternal gospel. This is why we can look to Elijah: his life points us to Jesus. Elijah's gospel is ours. This is true in three ways.

It is a gospel of repentance. Elijah's message to all of Israel was to turn from idols, sin, and turn back to God. He sought to persuade them to action. This word of repentance is the first word of the gospel. It was the first word out of Jesus' mouth at the start of his public ministry (Matt 4.17) and the first word from John's. We are exhorted, *'Repent, and believe the gospel.'*

John the Baptist is not a figure that we can relegate to the Old Testament era. Jesus said, *'the Law and the Prophets prophesied until John.'* To communicate the gospel, we need a prophetic word of repentance. We need the echo of an Elijah, of a John in our witness.

This is more than regret. A man or woman may look back and regret their sins and the consequences of their foolishness. But to be saved, a person must turn. It can be much easier for a church leader to get the congregation critiquing the faults of power structures, politicians, or big business rather than repenting of their own sin. Repentance involves realising that our deeds are evil and that they have offended a holy God. Only this produces the deep contrition that one needs to be fully born again by God's Spirit.

When we preach, we not only confront people with the truth about who God is, but we seek to persuade them to turn to that God. Elijah appeals to the crowd's reason, *'If Baal is God serve him. If Yahweh is God, serve him.'*

It is a gospel of atoning sacrifice. The Elijah ministry does more than issue a call to turn from sin. It's a call to turn to Christ. The climax of John the Baptist's ministry was in saying *'Behold the Lamb of God that takes away the sin of the world.'* Elijah himself also points us to Christ at the climax of his revival ministry on Mount Carmel. There he called down divine fire upon the mountain to consume a sacrifice that he had made for Israel's sins. He did this so that the hearts of God's people might be turned to Him.

And this points us to the gospel. Jesus said in John 3, *'when I am lifted, I will draw all men unto me.'* His sacrifice will turn people's hearts to God. But what sort of sacrifice will this be? It will be a sacrifice like Elijah's. Jesus says in Luke 12 *'I am come to bring fire to the earth—and how I wish it were already kindled! I have a baptism to be baptised with—and how constrained I am till it is accomplished!'* Using typical Hebrew parallelism, he repeats the same thing in a different way for effect. He speaks of a baptism of suffering and of bringing fire to the earth. What does he mean by this?

The fire and baptism are one in the same. He speaks of the Cross. In his sacrifice, he brings the fires of divine judgement upon himself. The fires and fury of God's violent punishment against sin descend upon the sacrifice. Jesus is offered the cup of hell and he empties it. He drinks damnation dry.

As we repent of and battle against the immorality of our day, we must always avoid moralism. We do not preach a world of good guys and bad guys. We are all bad guys and the one good guy was a sacrifice for us all. We do not preach the potential of human goodness. Our good deeds cannot erase our guilt before heaven. Only Jesus saves us from the coming wrath. Liberal theologians that are not centred on the Cross may see the fabrics of moralism as lovely and sophisticated serviettes to place on their philosophical dining tables. But, in reality, it is only Satan's personal menstrual rags they're wiping with.

It is a gospel of weakness. Like Jesus, Elijah chooses what looked like weakness. He chooses to be up north in Baal territory. He chooses a high mountain, the place of the Baals. He chooses a test well suited to Baal as a lightning god. He has given Baal all the advantages. To finish it off, Elijah handicaps himself by offering up his sacrifice in complete weakness by drenching it in water. Surely the Baalites thought Elijah was mad. They were spiritually insane, but not stupid. They knew that wet stuff did not burn.

But then the fire falls like a small, tactical nuke. The weakness of the sacrifice invites the power of God. Jesus' sacrifice also seemed like an act of weakness to the world. It was an impossible act. Yet God's power is made perfect in weakness—both in the weakness of Elijah's sacrifice as well as the in the cross. Elijah's story is our gospel: God saves through what looks to be ultimate weakness and ultimate folly.

Christians in revival are accordingly found living in God's presence (Coram Deo), attending to His Word, feeling acute concern about sin and righteousness, rejoicing in the assurance of Christ's love and their own salvation, spontaneously constant in worship, and tirelessly active in witness and service, fuelling these activities by praise and prayer.

- J.I. Packer

The Fire Falls

'Then fire fell from Heaven' -1Kg 18

Our generation needs more than just a theological explanation of God's power. We need a demonstration of that power. John said that Jesus would baptise his followers in the Holy Spirit and in fire. There are different types of fire in the Bible. We can be baptised in God's empowering holy fire because Jesus experienced the fire of judgment on the Cross. The great need of our day is men and women filled with this fiery power to reach a world sinking in hellfire.

God's messengers have spoken with tongues of supernatural fire since ancient times and all the more since the outpouring at Pentecost. In a generation filled with so much fake teaching, it is the holy flame that must adorn our gospel message. We need the Ghost.

Elijah prays down fire from heaven. It falls like a small grade nuclear weapon. The stones and the sacrifice, drenched in water, burst into searing flame. Only a living God could do such a thing. The people collapse face down in repentance. God has always been glorious. He has always been a consuming fire. He has always been the true and living God. But in this moment, His glory is manifest on earth.

On a cloudy day, the sun is still there. It is shining in all its brilliance. But we can't see it. Only when the clouds disperse, can we begin to see the sun burning. The book of Acts is like a long version of the Mt. Carmel event. A bunch of men in weakness—with little formal education or financial and political backing—go out to face the colossal strongholds of Rabbinic Judaism and Imperial Rome. And what do they do? They turn the world upside down. How? They offer up themselves as living sacrifices and they get clothed with fiery power from a living God.

We need more than just exegetical excellence and systematic soundness—as good as they are. We need the God of the resurrection to come and dwell among us and work with us in the preaching of the gospel. As it came on Mt. Carmel and as it came in Acts, this power comes when

God's men pray in faith. The 19th Century London preacher, Charles Spurgeon, says all this better than my amateurish fingers could ever type:

We need a work of the Holy Spirit of a supernatural kind,
putting power into the preaching of the Word, inspiring all believers with
heavenly energy, and solemnly affecting the hearts of the careless, so that they
turn to God and live. We would not be drunk with the wine of carnal excitement,
but we would be filled with the Spirit. We would behold the fire descending from
heaven in answer to the effectual fervent prayers of righteous men. Can we not
entreat the Lord our God to make bare His holy arm in the eyes of all the people in
this day of declension and vanity?

If part of our preparation for writing, blogging, sharing, or preaching the gospel does not involve time on our face getting this power, then we are still men who trust in the arm of the flesh—our own abilities, cleverness, and powers. What people need to see, is fire.

It is in the closet, with the door shut, that the sound of abundance of rain will first be heard.

- Andrew Murray

The Rain Maker

'He bowed down on the ground and put his face between his legs.' -1Kg 18

Hands stained with blood from the slaughter of counterfeit clergy, his labours are not yet done. There remains that little matter of the national drought. He lumbers over the still warm corpses and up out of the Wadi Kishon. Battering Baal's blaspheming bishops does work up a ravenous appetite. But there will be no food for Elijah. Instead, he considerately sends Ahab to go feast while he reclimbs the mountain and engages in his life's highest calling. He prays.

We've all had long days. Elijah has just had one. He has twice climbed a mountain, confronted a legion of raunchy rectors, preached a message that his life depended upon, built an altar with 12 large stones, persuaded a hostile crowd, called up faith to see a world-class miracle, and then led the repentant crowd to execute 450 of the playboy prophets.

It's probably stupid o' clock. But his day is not done. He must pray yet again for the nation he has owned in intercession for untold years. Elijah postures his body to reflect his spirit's cry and begins to call on God to complete the promise he has already begun to fulfil.

Prayer is not just meditative. It is priestly too. We do not engage in prayer just for ourselves, but to bring blessing to others as well. Though tired, Elijah prays. At first, there is no rain. He tries again. No rain. How long will he have to do this? He called out three times to Yahweh to see the dead boy raised. Third time? Nope, no rain.

If anyone would've ever been justified in ceasing prayers for a meal or a nap, it would be Elijah. But he will not give up. He will have God fulfil His promise to shower down blessing, or he will die asking. There is no giving up. After seven times of prayer, it is reported that a tiny cloud is coming. He has his answer.

Elijah is once again a small picture of Christ. Christ not only wins victory over the powers of darkness through his bloody sacrifice on the cross. But he then ascends to heaven where he makes intercession for us and rains on us the gift of the Holy Ghost.

We receive Christ's work. At first, we are only repentant Ahabs—feasting on the reward he has won for us. Christ is the hero, and we humbly receive the benefits. Our Christian life starts there, but it is not the whole story. We are transformed into his image as we partake of his life. We begin to learn to walk in the way of the prophets and the apostles, with Jesus being the chief cornerstone. We begin to, not only reap the benefits of his intercession, but also join him in bringing blessing to the world. We all start by receiving undeserved blessing. This causes us to grow into disciples, ones that give blessing as well.

There's no record of Jesus' followers ever asking him how to preach. But they did ask him how to pray. We learn to pray when we confess that we suck at it. God then begins to give us a spirit of intercession. We ask for a prayer life until we get one. God likes it when we get stubborn on our knees.

Are you ready to attend the Spirit's University? There are things you will learn in prayer about God that you cannot learn at a University. You can have more degrees than a hot day in Saudi Arabia and still have a frozen spirit. But you cannot be an ardent student at Prayer Uni and avoid catching the divine flame. There are many pulpits filled by men that have big heads and but tiny hearts. Yes, learning orthodox theology is of importance. But there are some things about God that are caught, not taught. They are caught in prayer as his Spirit imparts truths to our spirit. Yes, we read books. But Satan is a well-read theologian and he's none the better for it.

Our church needs more than men who just fill a pulpit or a blog with sound statements. It was said of the great London preacher Charles Spurgeon that, though his preaching was unequalled in his generation, it was when he prayed from the pulpit that the people were lifted into heaven. We may not all get a chance to have a big platform before men. But our platform before God can be as large as we make it. Not all of us have speaking or writing gifts, but faith is the great equaliser of humanity. It is in the prayer closet where we all have equal opportunity to 'ask the Father'—though we do not all take equal advantage of it.

If our generation is going to see revival and reformation, it will be because men set themselves to call down spiritual rain upon a dry land and pray until it comes.

Intimidation

'Jezebel sent a message to Elijah. Elijah was afraid.' -1Kg 19

Elijah has just experienced a spiritual high. He has given everything spiritually, psychologically, and emotionally. And after his quick, marathon run to Jezreel, he is sure to be physically exhausted as well. It is into this post-high Jezebel sends one of her most potent arrows: a message. Now, a message may not sound very scary, but messages are made of words. And if you remember, it was words that made our world. Words still make people's worlds. And when they are words sent by a witch and laced with intimidation, it can create a very fearful world for the unprepared heart. Elijah, who has not yet recharged his own soul after that huge battle, is devastated by it.

Intimidation also goes by the term *'fear of man'* in the Scriptures. It is sneaky. It can come from different or unexpected directions. Perhaps only a day had passed since Elijah stood boldly before 850 fake priests and soldiers that wanted him dead. Now he is terrified by one woman's message. Intimidation is something we constantly need to guard against as we can become vulnerable if we are not walking with the Master. Elijah was tired after having given so much, and he apparently let his guard down. After his moment of success, fear drives him down south, away from where God wants him to be.

Intimidation from the world can be a force that silences the preaching of the church. It can cause us to redefine what our calling truly is and embrace a fake, humanistic mission. Yes, giving out teddy bears, recycling, and weeding gardens is all good (and we should do such things) but our primary calling is to boldly preach the message of repentance and forgiveness. Intimidation can redirect that ultimate focus towards a more socially acceptable goal.

For example, we can think of churches that have publicly taken up the cause of human trafficking. Great! This should be opposed by all Christians. But this battle is socially acceptable. The world applauds when we fight trafficking. 200 years ago, when William Wilberforce and his crew fought against slavery in the British Empire, not too many people cheered. Likewise, how many of these same churches are also willing to publicly enter the fight for the rights of unborn children? That is a social justice issue that is not so trendy.

Jezebel not only works through aggressive third-wave Feminist organisations or bullying LGBT activist groups with big budgets. It can also be in the church. These Jezebel principles can work through a man or woman. If you are a leader in the church, who is the person you are terrified to confront over internal issues? Does your heart start inexplicably beating with anxiety when you get a text message from a particular person even before you have read it? The person may be a Christian. They may not be consciously manipulative. But the enemy is somehow using intimidation to paralyse you.

What people or groups intimidate you? People in church? People in society? Your spouse? Family? Who is it you need to rely on God for strength in order to address?

After what seems like ministry victories and spiritual advances, look for the pushback. It may come as an email, a text message, a verbal comment, or something on social media. Jezebel will send you anything that will keep you from progressing in personal godliness or church ministry. She will seek to paralyse your activity with confusion, anxiety or depression so that you don't travel further into her territory. When this happens, recognise her work, realise the battle is spiritual (not against flesh and blood), pray, and keep going.

Zealous for The Name

'I have been very zealous for Yahweh my God.' -1Kg 19

Elijah rollercoasters through his generation in ways that often rob us of breath. It does not read like a boring life. And though we 21st century Westerners might find some of the events unsavoury (the slaughter of Baal's vile vicars, calling down fire on soldiers, etc), they are nonetheless straightforward and easy to understand.

But chapter 19 continually causes confusion for readers and is something of a conundrum for commentators. Godly teachers disagree about how we should understand this bit of the narrative. The chapter raises lots of questions. Does Yahweh send Elijah to Horeb? Is he going of his own accord? Why is he running from Jezebel? Is Yahweh's whisper to be understood as a correction—or merely as further instruction? And Elijah's comment about being the only prophet? Should that be seen as pride?

Brains far more exercised than mine have attempted to answer these questions and come to different conclusions. My unhallowed fingers dare not dance across these laptop keys to try and address those ambiguities in the Biblical story. But not all is unclear in this chapter. There are elements in this episode that speak without confusion to all our simple ears—if we'll listen.

The repeated claim that Elijah has been *'jealous for Yahweh my God'* is one of those elements. It hits our conscious like a hammer. It reflects a way of thinking that, though straightforward, is alien to our culture. We can feel the force of this statement because it is driving in the opposite direction to the one we as a society have been travelling towards for some time—and our collision with the statement is jarring.

We don't know all that is going on in Elijah's head in this chapter, but it is likely that this statement by Elijah is inspired by something that Yahweh once said to Moses on this very same mountain. *'You shall worship no other gods, for Yahweh, whose name is Jealous, is a jealous God.'* Huh? What does it even mean for us to be jealous for our God?

God will tell Ezekiel a couple of hundred years later that '*I will be zealous for my own Holy name.*' Is the mission of our church built around a zeal to faithfully reflect and proclaim the name of God to our world? Do we grieve when we hear God misrepresented in sermons? Do we have a sense of loyalty to proclaim who God is from Scripture—even when it seemingly conflicts with the theological and ideological systems we are surrounded by?

The most precious thing that Elijah can give his generation is not oil, flour, or even rain. It is the knowledge of what the one, living God is like. We do not need inquisitors to suppress fake teaching in the darkness of a backroom. We need teachers who are willing to boldly expose it with the sunlight of Scripture. Paul exhorts Timothy '*watch your life and doctrine closely.*' Keeping ourselves morally clean is only half the work. We must test the teaching we believe with Scripture and be open to correction. We cannot afford to give the world a corrupt gift and present a fake god wrapped up in Christian terms or religiosity. We cannot give them an Asherah that drags in Yahweh's clothes.

Mother God?

'Zealous for the name of God.' -1Kg 19

'A child who has been taught to pray to a Mother in Heaven would have a religious life radically different from that of a Christian child.' -CS Lewis

As we are speaking of Elijah's zeal for the name of God, it is worth highlighting an increasingly relevant issue for our generation. It is the growing tendency to refer to God as *She*. It is fair to say that this subject triggers a lot of people. When discussed online, this issue of *Mama God* tends to bring out the angry emojis, the exclamation marks, AND WORST OF ALL THE CAPS LOCK.

Some Feminist theologians say this feminine title is a good trend. Why do they say it is? One of the reasons they give is that the Bible was written in 'patriarchal' days. It is argued: *in rugged Old Testament times, the idea of a female God would never have been accepted. We can accept that God is equally masculine and feminine now that we are more enlightened and so our terms should reflect that.* Or so the reasoning goes. But there is an invalid presupposition here. You may have already picked up on it. History shows us that the Bible's use of exclusively masculine titles for God is not part of a wider woman-hating phenomenon that was part of the Ancient Near East (ANE). Israel was countercultural by NOT having a high female deity. Having God only as a Father or King was unique.

Elijah faces both Baal and Asherah on the mountain. Having a maternal and paternal deity to oversee and spawn lesser powers was a normal part of the ANE cosmology. And not all goddesses were hyper-sexualised. In surrounding culture 'Tiamat' was seen as the maternal deity that begets other powers before time begins. Other high female deities existed at this time as well and feminine titles were normal—especially that of 'mother'.

'You are Mother and Father of all that you made.'-Akhenaten, Short Hymn
'I have no mother - you are my Mother!' – Gudea

Referring to God exclusively as *King* and *Father* (never the titles *Queen* or *Mother*) was not due to Israel being a product of its day. Rather, it showed that they were radically counter-cultural. The same could be said of the

Greco-Roman world in which the New Testament was written. In the 1st Century, Hera sat with her husband Zeus at the top of the divine pyramid of power. It would have been very normal to refer to the divine as 'she' in Ephesus where deity was so strongly feminine—but St. Paul never did.

Others propose that we refer to God as 'Mother' due to the fact that both men and women are created in his image. We both certainly are. But this argument presupposes that God is referred to as a man in the Bible. He is not. He is referred to as Father. And He was a Father before He made humans. Calling Him 'Father' is not the same as calling Him male.

Others argue for the use of 'Mother' for more pastoral reasons. They rightly point out that some have a cold, distant, or even abusive fathers. They do not want people to project those associations onto God and so they propose that the term 'Mother' be used in such cases.

But this only begs the question: what if the person has a bad relationship with their mother too? Do we then go on to the next or the warmest familial relationship? Could we give God the titles of Uncle, Auntie, or Little Sister if those relationships hold the warmest emotive quality for us? Though it may be rooted in the best of intentions, it becomes a therapeutic idolatry.

Some may argue that referring to God as Father somehow gives men a holier place than women. They claim the exclusive use of 'Father' reinforces 'The Patriarchy' (ill-defined as that term may be) and allows men to relate better to God than women. But does experience really lead us to believe that sons are always closer to their father than daughters are? Don't we know daughters that have close and affectionate relationships with their fathers as well as sons who have strained relationships with them?

I have two sons and two daughters. I am not any closer to my sons because we share the same gender. My daughters do not need to refer to me as 'mother' in order to be close to me. If we adopt Feminist reasoning, aren't there are other terms in Scripture that might make it harder for men to relate? The church is referred to as the Bride of Christ. Some men may have trouble relating to that. Not all men can see themselves in a white dress. Should we call the church Christ's 'Husband' to help them? After all, we don't really believe the church has a specific gender. Do we? Is it not all metaphorical anyway? A spouse is a spouse regardless of gender. Right?

No. God never reveals himself with a feminine title in Scripture. Some may point out metaphors that have feminine connotations—but that is quite a different thing. God compares his love for Israel in the Psalms to the love of a hen for her chicks. But a title is never imparted. The metaphor does not mean we should call God 'Mother' any more than we should call Him 'Chicken'.

European revolutionary ideas of equality may lead us to call God 'Mother' - but this is not a choice rooted in Scripture. It is our cultural upbringing that pushes us in this direction. There is not a lot about equality in the Bible in the sense that some seem to want. God chooses some for one purpose, but not others. To some, he assigns the task of being the eyes of the body, to others as being the ears.

As clever as we think we are, we do not have the right to pick new titles for God because they seem right to us. He chooses to reveal Himself in the ways He thinks best. Jesus—in whom the full expression of God was revealed—only ever called God 'Father', never 'Mother'. He did not do that because he was a limited product of his culture. If Jesus' example does not fit in with our theological idealism, then it is our theology - not the Scriptures - that need to change.

To look back upon the progress of the divine Kingdom upon earth is to review revival periods which have come like refreshing showers upon dry and thirsty ground, making the desert to blossom as the rose, and bringing new eras of spiritual life and activity just when the Church had fallen under the influence of the apathy of the times.

- E.M. Bounds

#ElijahMen

Disillusionment & Loneliness

'It is enough; now, O Lord, take away my life.' -1Kg 19

Elijah is depressed. At the very least, he is in a funk to the point of no longer wanting to be alive. Like a lot of mental health sufferers, it seems so illogical to outsiders: *didn't Elijah just have a major victory? Doesn't he have a lot to be thankful for? Why isn't he happy?* Sometimes our internal pains make sense. Sometimes they do not.

We find Elijah under the tree and he is so disillusioned that he wants to die. Many of us have been there at least once in life—maybe twice. Maybe more. Few things wound a man like disillusionment even though we may mentally acknowledge that the removal of our illusions is good for us.

I write this on the Saturday before Easter. Some have called it '*Long Saturday*' or '*Silent Saturday*'. It is the Saturday when the disciples were hurt and confused. The circumstantial drama of the crucifixion was over. The joy of Easter had not yet begun. The wound had been delivered. Now they were processing their pain.

Disillusionment is a particular type of mental suffering. It is the effect of unmet expectations and disappointments amplified. Sometimes disillusionment is in the form of circumstances: the ideal job you wanted is not what you thought it would be. Sometimes it is in the quality of our churches: the people and leadership have a far more toxic culture than you ever anticipated. And other times it is in a relationship: a close family member or friend is not there for you in the way that they promised they would be. They may be suddenly gone. Or, you may realise the relationship was not at all what you thought it was. That is hard.

We men fall to pieces so quietly at times. We hurt—but no one knows or understands how. At times, God allows his men to undergo this baptism of darkness. A minister of a previous generation once said that before God can use a man mightily, he must first wound him mightily. Perhaps. Sadly, Elijah's loner ways have caught up with him, and there is no one around to encourage or comfort him. He goes through this valley with no human companionship.

This loneliness seems to be as much a dynamic in Elijah's breakdown as the disillusionment. Elijah tells God twice that '*I alone am left*'. That is not quite true of course. But it is how we feel at times. Loneliness is a cancer. It has destroyed far more Christians than homosexuality ever will. This spectre sneaks up on you and drops a surprise kiss on your soul like a fart from hell. It festers. Pastors suffer more than most—often unconsciously so. Spiritual leadership on that level is isolating, especially when most of the people you serve don't understand what your job actually entails. Many come to you with their problems, but who do you go to with yours?

In this book, we focus a lot on pornography and LGBT ideology. We haven't said much about the adultery of pastors even though that has been hugely devastating to many. There are a couple of reasons for that. The first is that there are currently no high-profile religious leaders writing books and giving talks about how it is morally acceptable for a pastor to commit adultery. We are not being asked to affirm them in their transgression. We all know it is wrong, even though it happens. If a pastor is found to be having an affair, he is removed. (Unless he has an affair with another man. Then he is applauded for coming out—depending on his denomination.)

Pastors do not have affairs because they are encouraged to by fake teaching. They usually do not even have them out of lust—most ministers don't have that level of energy! The majority of pastors who have had affairs have done so because they are lonely. They have a lack of healthy friendships, or an unhealthy marriage, or both. This is true of many Christian men, but especially pastors. For such a man, the affair is not the primary problem. It is the fake medication for the primary problem. Always encourage your pastor to take time away from 'church work' to invest in healthy relationships where he can be poured into. Your pastor probably pours out far more to you and your congregation than he gets poured into.

The author of 1 Kings does not give us a full report on how Elijah slipped into this unfortunate state. After all, he had just performed a mighty miracle and won a decisive victory over the false religious teachers. Many of his countrymen turned to God as a result. Isn't the success of revival supposed to make you feel better? He now has fans and a huge social media following—*how could he be lonely*?

If only.

But in spite his victory, this is where we find Elijah. Everything was building towards the confrontation at Mt. Carmel. And now it is over. It is a bit like how many people experience the intense build up to Christmas, only to feel empty once the celebrations are finished. Now Elijah is left wondering if his greatest moment is past. What else is on life's radar? What do we do when the glory is gone and we are left with nothing but good memories? How long will this darkness last? What is there to live for?

It is impossible to see Easter morning when you are in Silent Saturday—but it is coming. God is now doing his silent work in the confusion and the pain. You are treading paths that God's men have plodded along for centuries. Keep being faithful. Be obedient to what God has given you to do. Invest in your relationship with Him and in healthy, honest relationships with brothers and sisters. God's grace often comes through letting other saints speak to us in our vulnerability.

We may think our story in God has tragically ended. In reality, He's merely preparing us for the next chapter.

The Whisper

'After the fire, was the soft whisper.' -1Kg 19

Much has been made of the divine whisper that Elijah hears on Horeb and not all of it is fit for consumption. Some commentators get mindlessly mystical over this.

An earthquake, a wind, and a fire all come upon the mountain. But God speaks in none of them. Finally, God speaks to Elijah in the form of a whisper. He asks what he is doing there and then sends him back up to Israel with further instructions.

Those who run meditation retreat centres tend to jump all over this one. *See, God isn't in the big, loud, and dramatic elements of life. He's in the place of silence and solitude.* Now, it is true that God often speaks to us in the quiet. It is also the experience of many Christians that it is healthy for us to regularly step away from our busy routines, calm ourselves, and be alone with God.

But there is a large leap we must take from saying that God *can* speak in the whisper to saying that God *always* speaks in the whisper or even that silent solitude is His preferred method of speaking. There exists, in our strange world of Churchianity, certain contemplative Pharisees who despise the big and the loud simply because it is big and loud and who take great pride in how many hours they can be silently aloof. Now as an introvert myself, I get this. I welcome quiet times alone. In fact, I thrive on them. But is this always the place where God shows up? Does He never show up in crowds or in relationships with other humans? Is He never noisy?

The episode on Horeb is not there to teach us that God always speaks in the whisper. It teaches us that God often speaks in ways that we do not expect. In the chapter before, God showed up in the fire. When Elijah leaves this life, it will not be a whisper that takes him up to heaven, but a whirlwind. When God confirms the work of His Son on the cross, He doesn't send down a whisper, He sends an earthquake. At Pentecost, God births the church in wind and flame. God's character is steadfast. But when it comes to His methods, we should be alert as we don't know how He is going to move.

This is important for us to keep in mind both for our personal lives and for the church. When we pray for reform, we are praying for specific changes that we see which need addressing in the church. We may rightfully have a specific vision of what that change will look like. We know what Scripture says and we see where we have erred as a people.

But when we pray for revival as well, we are praying for a fresh injection of spiritual vitality into our lethargic souls. And God tends to answer those prayers in ways we do not always expect. Jesus said '*the wind blows where it will and we don't know where it comes from or where it is going. So are those led by the Spirit.*' The Ghost tends to keep us on our toes. When a fresh awakening comes to a spiritually sleepy nation, it may come through a church, a denomination, a minister, or a style of worship that is not our favourite. Sometimes grace offends. God may show up in a way that is as far from our expectations as a whisper is from an earthquake.

I, Ahab.

Vile toad of a male
squatted on a fading throne
yields to intimidation
permits to be
what should not
where God has given a mantle to lead.
The royal toad is me
when I feed
my body's appetites
neglecting my spirit.
It's **not** a particular personality.
It **is** a corrupt character.
The zeitgeist whispers Jezebellic
deception in one ear
God proclaims Elijahian
truth in the other.
At times
truth feels as cosy
as a jackhammer
One that shatters fetters.
But I love my chains.
Slavery is my comforting blanket.
Sin's whisper tickles
ears and appears to us
a thing of dreams
while the serpent subtly gnaws.
Can't reform the world
if my soul is unreformed.

Elisha and the Accountability Police

*'Go back. What have I done for you?' -*1Kg 19

Elijah comes back from his wanderings in the desert and calls Elisha to be his disciple. He responds with zeal, lights a BBQ, and the whole village eats lots of meat. Wonderful. Elijah will now no longer be travelling alone. In addition, a group who hears about Elijah's exploits against Baal's blasphemy bishops begin to gather around him in hopes of catching some of his spiritual power. There are at least fifty of them—probably more. But one gets the impression that Elijah may not be fully wild over his new fam. Our preacher prefers to be alone and having a tribe around—while good for him—may not be what he's most comfortable with. Elijah is not exactly Mr Social. Fortunately, Elisha seems to have more people skills and helps to lead this school with him.

It is important to note something about Elijah's relationship with Elisha. Elijah is reluctant about having this mini-me follow him around. From the first time we see them together to the moment just before Elijah soars up to heaven, he seems to want his mentee to back off so that he can retreat back into his private cave. Elijah takes on a mentee—and the growing school—out of obedience to God, not out of preference. His goal has always been to see Yahweh glorified and not to build a following for himself.

There's a couple of important lessons for us here, not least of which is obedience to the call. After all, doing ministry doesn't always mean doing whatever you like doing. But something else is relevant to those of us in the 21st Century British church. Elijah comes across as a strong alpha-male. Nothing is wrong with that. We certainly need such men in the church right now. But there is a common pitfall among alpha-males: they often like to control others. Holding Elijah up superficially could, at first, draw in the type of men who like to have people under their leadership and some newer quarters of the UK church have experienced this. Some newer churches have had unhealthy expressions of accountability, sometimes under banners with titles such as 'apostolic leadership'.

Now the Bible does talk about accountability. It speaks of leaders being accountable for actions they take, how they handle money, etc. But in some churches, an unhealthy culture has grown up where everyone is expected to be personally accountable to the pastors or elders. Many of us know tragic cases where leaders have demanded too much authority in people's personal lives. When church members seem hesitant to submit, they are accused of having *'trust issues'* or *'a rebellious spirit'*. Such leaders—usually with a faux-humble veneer—regularly check on members to make sure they are submitting.

On a personal note, one church in a city where I once worked had a long trail of people who had bled out, being spiritually abused by the alpha-male lead pastor. It was one of the saddest things I have ever witnessed happening in the name of Christ. Yes, as a pastor I understand the temptation. Not everyone in our churches always does what we would like, and that makes it hard to lead. But Scripture is clear—we lead by example, not by *'lording it over them'*.

Elijah never demands submission or personal loyalty from those who follow him. Many choose to freely give it. But ironically, Elijah often tries to give it back. This is a healthy spiritual relationship. The mentee should be chasing the mentor more than vice versa. Loyalty that is freely given to a mentor can be a beautiful thing as long as it does not eclipse one's loyalty to Christ himself. In the end, Elisha's personal loyalty to Elijah is rewarded with a double portion. He never abandons his mentor—even if his mentor wishes he would at times. This is never a loyalty that Elijah tries to call forth or manipulate like some alpha-male church leaders do. He does not need people to need him. Loyalty should be freely given, not guilt tripped into. Ultimately, we are Christ's sheep and we must hear and follow his voice above any man's.

Elisha is also wise in how he relates to his mentor. He knows what he is supposed to be imitating and what he is not—a fine discrimination that many enthusiastic mentees lack. Elisha is zealous to be around Elijah and to catch his spiritual flame, but he doesn't take on Elijah's personality. We have no indication that he started dressing like him, telling the same sort of jokes, or listening to the same type of music. Yes, Elisha did pick up a lot from Elijah. He got the powerful gift of prophecy and a profound sense of God's holiness. Like Elijah, he also develops a spiritually healthy friendship with a woman—this time a married one. And, the most well-known of all, he developed faith for the working of miracles of both mercy and judgement.

But Elisha did not lose his own identity and personality. We see Elijah hanging out in the wilderness. Elisha, by contrast, is often found in towns. Elijah is an introvert. Elisha is seemingly an extrovert and is often in groups. Elijah confronted rulers. Elisha conversed with them. Elisha was more international. We are in a healthy mentoring relationship when we know exactly what we want to catch from the person we choose to draw near to. Perhaps we desire to mature in our prayer life, our friendships, our Bible study, or our evangelism. We find someone to mentor us in that particular area, but not necessarily in others. We are not to be their clones.

This tendency to over imitate is particularly noteworthy in our generation as we have such an epidemic of fatherlessness. Some people may want a strong mentor figure simply to fill an emotional need and it is altogether unclear what is being imparted. Yes, the body of Christ can fill emotional voids with its familial nature—we can think of Paul with Timothy. Relational affection may well grow in a mentoring relationship. But disciple-making in itself is not quite the same thing as being part of a redemptive family. Though we may be zealous to be near a spiritual father, we do not want to lose our identity by copying them in every respect. We are not to make ourselves subservient to our mentors in an unhealthy or idolatrous way.

This holds true on the horizontal level, among brothers, as well. Yes, we need those who will speak truth to us in love. We all have our blind spots and sometimes need to hear hard truths. But we are not simply to be accountability police who go after each other when we see sin or immaturity. In the body of Christ, we should aim to be known for our encouragement and comfort more than our correction or rebuke. There will always be some who want to tear down more than build up. Let us be careful with terms like 'accountability partners'. We are called into a community of friends. We build healthy relationships where we can express honest concern and not just get paired up to police each other's behaviour.

Elijah reluctantly accepts an enthusiastic Elisha—a relationship defined by freedom, not control.

Petition God for the Holy determination and bravery you must have to follow Christ. Without it, you cannot be what you profess.

-William Gurnall, 1655

God Coaches the Coward

'Let not the one who puts on armour boast like one who takes it off.' -1Kg 20

I am a beta-male by nature. By that I mean I try to avoid conflict, am content to dwell within my own imaginative world, and have no grand aspirations to lead crowds. I am not the naturally aggressive type, not the guy who aims to be captain of the football team, nor one who has been destined as a risk-taking CEO since he was seven. In the words of Bilbo Baggins—and I can relate to Hobbits only too well—'*Adventures make one late for dinner'*.

Ahab is an unsanctified beta whose lack of spiritual leadership is ruining the kingdom he is supposed to be leading. He often seems to have all the backbone of a chocolate éclair. But God loves Ahab. And here God puts him in a hellish situation where he is forced to grow a pair and lead his people into a conflict he would rather avoid. God often does this to men He loves.

It all begins when the King of Aram, Ben-Hadad, gathers his forces and lays siege to Samaria, the capital city. Ahab has three options: he can try to endure the siege, go out and fight the army, or bow the knee to Ben-Hadad and become his vassal. Now Ahab knows these are vicious blokes, so he chooses the easiest of the three. He cowers before the bully's overwhelming army and sends a messenger out to say that everything the King is and has now belongs to Aram's King. Voila, conflict avoided.

But God doesn't let Ahab off the hook that easily. He forces him to step into his fears. Ben-Hadad sends the messenger back to Ahab and says that his vassal's pledge will be put to the ultimate test the very next day. He will come through the castle and take everything that he sees that he likes—not just in principle (as was often the case in such surrenders) but in actual fact. This King doesn't just want Israel's submission. He wants its humiliation. Ahab knows that he cannot allow such a thing, but he is too scared to act decisively. He calls for the elders to counsel him. They all agree that he cannot allow Aram to do this to Israel. Ahab is forced to send a refusal, though he words it in the most deferential way possible. Predictably, the

King of Aram says that this answer is not acceptable and that he will destroy Samaria.

Finally, God has Ahab right where wants him. He must fight. Remember, that this episode happens shortly after Elijah's revival meeting on Mt. Carmel. Repentance has happened. Grace is in the air. And we see that manifesting in this moment. Instead of wetting himself on the spot, Ahab gets to say one of the manliest one-liners in all of Scripture. His reply to the bully-king is short: *Let not him who puts on his armour boast like the one who takes it off!*

Notice how in this story Jezebel is not mentioned once. She seems to have temporarily retreated into the background—even if for a season. Ahab does not ask her counsel on how to handle Aram. He goes to the elders for that. Jezebel makes men weak. And now that Ahab has set his face to battle, an unnamed prophet of Yahweh emerges and steps into the court. This is one of the effects of Elijah's breakthrough. Yahweh's prophets are no longer being hunted. They once again have access to speak to the throne. A resurgence of preachers is visible in the land, seeking to reform and revive the apostate nation.

This prophet of Yahweh is no pacifist. His God is the ultimate warrior. He encourages Ahab in his military stance and instructs him on how to engage Aram. But here is the catch: he needs to go out and strike first. He cannot sit back and wait to be overwhelmed. He must take the fight to the aggressors. And he does. In good King Théoden fashion, he has a Helms Deep moment and overwhelms the much larger army that has laid siege to his people.

Part of having discernment is to know when to make peace and when to fight. Our personalities and the effects of sin will give us a natural bent to either being too warlike or too passive and at usually all the wrong times. We need to know ourselves. If you are, like me and Ahab, a man who is naturally on cruise control and content to go with the flow, then be watchful. We do not know how this story would've played out had Ahab still been 100% under the influence of Jezebel. Perhaps she would've negotiated with the King of Aram directly and traded her husband for an upgraded queenly throne in Damascus. But because this was a season of life where he was open to hearing the prophetic word of God, Ahab had a victory.

Where is God calling you to fight? What areas of your life are crippled by passivity or anxiety? Do you see areas where God may be orchestrating circumstances to make you fight for what you know to be right? The opposition may look big, but our God often works through courageous men who fight in spite of the odds. God rescues those who wade into darkness for the glory of his name. Isn't this the heart of the gospel? Isn't it through the apparent weakness of the cross that God worked his victory over sin and death?

God's enemies may be on the aggressive march, but they have yet to take off their armour.

The Valley God

'Their God is a god of the mountains only.' -1Kg 20

Ahab performed a momentary and lacklustre repentance. Yet God in his mercy has responded to this and given Israel victory over Aram (Syria). We now encounter a bit of Ancient Near East theology. After this military upset, we hear the conversation of Aram's defeated generals with their King. To their credit, they are willing to examine the theological dimensions of a military exercise. But theology is not neutral nor consequence free. Bad theology is more than an abstraction. It leads to bad outcomes in what we materialistic folk like to confidently refer to as 'real life'.

Their reasoning was simple enough. Israel had won on a mountain—*and isn't Israel's god all into mountains?* They had some reason for assuming so. Israel's law was given through Moses on a mountain. These generals may also have heard about the national revival that happened on Mt. Carmel. Yahweh seems to dig mountains. *So why not fight the Israelis in the valleys instead? A god who is good on the mountains probably won't be any good in the valleys. Right?* This faux theological reasoning (so similar to the social media theology of our day) proves disastrous for the army. They go out to war again and Israel whips them like a rented mule there in the valley—just as they had done before in the mountains.

But in their defeat, some of the soldiers of Aram now know that *'Yahweh is God'*—just as the prophet said would happen. Even in God's temporal judgements, there is the goal of salvation through the knowledge of who He is.

We don't need to allow ourselves a super-sized portion of poetic license to relate to Syria's theological taboo. Aren't we guilty of similar patterns of thinking? Do we not tend to put God in certain spheres? Are there not times and seasons and ways where we think God will move—but not in others? Like Aram's generals, we expect God to answer prayers and show up in situations when we feel strong or when we have those mountaintop experiences with him.

But when we are in life's valleys, we often do not expect as much. Miraculous answers to prayer or the conversion of those around us are not something we expect when we feel God is far from us. And yet it's in the valleys where God tends to surprise us. Personally, when this author reflects on the last 20 years of serving the Lord, the three most fruitful seasons have come at times when it was least expected, and when there was much personal unhappiness. Sometimes God will use us the most when we feel the most reluctant to be used. If you are in a valley, press into God in prayer and step out in obedience—even if you cannot do so joyfully. God may just use you in your weakness for the glory of his name.

This story also speaks about who owns this world. It is His. There is not one square inch of this planet where Jesus does not look down from heaven and say, 'Mine!' France is his. Berlin is his. Japan is his. Mecca, Saudi Arabia is his. India is all his. This earth and all it contains is his. Neutrality is a myth. When we engage with atheists, Muslims, and people of other religions, the buildings that we meet in to do so always belong to Jesus. The gifts of reason and logic that we use in our discussions belongs to him. And the air that people breathe when they blasphemy his name is his.

The Cancer of Spiritual Pacifism

'He is my brother.' -1Kg 20

God gives Ahab an unexpected victory over the much superior army of the Syrian King, Ben-Hadad. They are vastly outnumbered and have far fewer resources. But God fights with them and the body count among the enemy soldiers is high. Syria's King flees and hides for his life, wondering how he will survive. Then one of his counsellors mentions how the rulers of Israel are *'merciful'* and this gives the king an idea.

A humble looking messenger is sent from Ben-Hadad to Ahab and the King agrees to receive his defeated foe. Ben-Hadad takes the passenger's seat in Ahab's chariot and he gets driven around town. The defeated Syrian king says, *'You can set up a market in our city and I'll return what my dad stole from your dad.'* Ahab is pleased by these concessions and lets him go free. For this, God speaks a harsh word of judgement over Ahab. He speaks this word through a prophet who goes to great lengths to dramatize his message including getting beat up and seeing a lion eat another prophet.

Why is God unhappy with Ahab? Isn't Ahab being kind and merciful to Ben-Hadad? Aren't God's men supposed to act like this? And what's with the lion eating the other prophet? Isn't God being rather harsh in this story?

No, God isn't being harsh—either with the King or with the disobedient prophet. He is judging righteously. Ahab fails to execute his duty before God. Aram is a danger to His people. They are cruel in their warfare—even ripping open pregnant women. God gave Ahab a miraculous victory over this much bigger power and now he has their very king. Ahab has all the bargaining chips. What does he do with these resources? He wastes them.

Ahab could have ensured his people's safety for generations to come. Instead, the King of Aram played him. He flattered him, calling this lesser Israeli King his 'brother'. Being used to being led by his wife, Ahab clearly wasn't used to feeling like a strong man. Now one of the most powerful Kings in that part of the world was being deferential to him. It must have felt great. But this is another test God's men must master. *We should learn how to accept human rejection. But we also must learn how to reject human acceptance.* Ahab gave Ben-Hadad his freedom in exchange for minuscule concessions in this ecstasy of being accepted by one of the strong leaders of his day.

What happens because of this? A generation later, Aram is once again butchering God's people. Ahab dropped the ball. Because he chooses to wine and dine with a big shot instead of ferociously fighting evil, Israeli children have to watch their fathers being tortured and their mothers raped. Allowing evil influences to roam free in the church (and sometimes the world) will have consequences. It is your job to use whatever authority God has given you to destroy what is destructive to his Body.

The Fight Club scene between the two prophets underscores this. We may agree that *'I want you to hit me as hard as you can'* is a rather peculiar request. Certainly, it is even more peculiar when this request is the Word of the Lord. But the prophet refuses to throw a punch. He is infected with spiritual pacifism. It is sin to strike when God says not to. But it is also a sin to not strike when God says we should. We show mercy to repentant or vulnerable people—not sin or fake teaching. With those we are ruthless.

A lack of spiritual aggression against the work of the devil is one of the chief sins of this generation of Christian men. When John wrote his epistle, he noted, *'I write to you young men because you are strong, the word of God lives in you, and you have overcome the evil one.'* Can this be said of the young men in our congregation? Of us?

Do we march with the songs of God in our mouth and holy violence in our hearts towards the demonic? Or, are we played by our pride? Do we relish being seen as sophisticated enough to make room for some things that are contrary to God's word? Are we flattered by compliments for our 'open-mindedness' or 'tolerance' by those whose affirmations we value? Or, are we committed to resisting evil in the spheres of our influence wherever we find it?

The Witch's Warming Whispers

'Be happy and eat something. I'll get it for you.' -1Kg 21

Ahab is moody again. Naboth won't sell the King his vineyard—a vineyard the King wants so he can have a bigger garden. Naboth is a righteous man and he won't trade his father's inheritance for money. What does Ahab do? He goes home and sucks his thumb. He didn't get the vineyard, but he still knows how to whine as much as any crushed grape. Life doesn't give him what he wants, so he indulges in the sin of pouting—a sin adults, as well as children, can be guilty of.

He tells his wife all about it. She will give him what he wants. She comforts his pouting and leaves his character in poverty. She is from Tyre where Kings are above the law—her daddy always got what he wanted. Now she will get her husband what he wants. All she has to do is throw a righteous man under the bus and her husband will get what he wants. *Hey, anything for the marriage.*

There have been many innocents down through the ages that have been sacrificed on the altar of love. When this love—marital or otherwise—becomes a god, it will then inevitably become a devil.

Men, don't marry a woman who cares more about your comfort than your character. If you choose to marry, then marry a woman who kicks your butt if you insist on unrighteous attitudes and actions. Ahab should've had a wife that challenged him to be righteous in his dealings with Naboth and not simply help feed his own immaturities. Search for a gal who will help you live godly—not one who will merely help you feel good. (This could be said of close friendships as well as marriage.) Sadly, our King didn't marry such a woman. He married one who excused his moodiness instead of confronting it.

But there is more instruction here than just who we marry or befriend. We are tempted to let ourselves go and anticipate comfort whenever Jezebel whispers in our ear that she will take care of us. But ultimately, she doesn't *take care of us*. At least not in the Julie Andrews sense of the phrase. If anything, she means it in more of an Al Pacino fashion. The bread and stolen waters she feeds us initially taste sweet, but they are poison. The whispers of the witch may warm our wounded ego, but it is only to bring about our own demise. She sings a lullaby to us while she prepares her cursed knife.

Always look out for self-pity. It makes us particularly susceptible to the manipulation of sin. It speaks to our ego: *'You deserve better than this'*, *'God wouldn't allow you to go through this pain'*, *'You deserve better than how your spouse treats you'*, *'You should be getting more recognition for your hard work and giftedness'*. Self-pity whispers to us about how unfair our life circumstances are until we repeat these phrases in agreement. Once it convinces us that we are not getting what we deserve—once we have fully adopted the victim mentality that it lulls us into—then it presents a way of escape. Temptation is most effective when it presents itself as a form of relief.

In contrast to self-pity, God calls his men to a life of thanksgiving and repentance. Men who live this way are constantly amazed at how much better God is being to them then they deserve. They are aware of their daily shortcomings and sins. They confess them to God and thank Him for the gift of forgiveness. They thank God for their daily food and mean it. They do not complain about not having the trendiest of shoes. They are too busy thanking God for the gift of two feet. Jezebel wants them to believe they deserve far better. But they refuse this attitude. Instead, they realise that God treats them with far more kindness than they have ever come close to meriting on their own. Every day is a gift. Even in life's hard season—and we all have valleys of pain—they can give thanks, for they do not walk those valleys alone.

We all need comfort at times. But true disciples go to God for their rest and refuse the fake medications of sinful comforts. These disciples attune their ears to God's healing voice and shut out worldly whispers by refusing self-pity. Their aim is not to nurture wounded pride. It's to kill it.

🖋

How to Give and Receive Hard Words

'So, you found me, my enemy.' -1Kg 21

Since the whole episode at Mt. Carmel, Elijah and Elisha have had a measure of freedom in their preaching work. After that mountainous revival hit, Baal's police-priests were slaughtered and public opinion partially turned against Jezebel's despotic religious agenda. Spiritual revival is turning into a more permanent expression of reform in some quarters. This is not to say that the nation has successfully repented. But a small bit of light is now shining and a faithful few are on the march. At least 50 preachers, known as 'the sons of the prophets', are in Elijah's tutelage and people are listening to them.

At this time, God calls Elijah to give a hard word to King Ahab. Ahab had ceased government-sponsored persecution of the prophets and had shown an openness—albeit a small one—to Yahweh's prophetic word since their last encounter. Elijah had at least some reason to be encouraged that his prayers for Ahab were taking effect. But now God has given him a hard word and, as a messenger, he must be obedient to give it whether he wants to or not. Love without truth is mere sentimentalism.

Jezebel has killed a righteous man. The most blasphemous Queen that Israel has ever known had Naboth run through a kangaroo court and executed on fake charges of blasphemy. The irony is dark as are the days. Like many of her spiritual daughters throughout the ages, Jezebel executed her agenda by wrapping it all up in a religious veneer. She called for a time of fasting and asked for the charge to be confirmed by two (fake) witnesses in accordance with Mosaic law. Etiquette is etiquette. Especially in religion. *If we are going to murder an innocent, let's do so properly.* Evil can be impressively civilised.

The means of execution was the slow, painful death of stoning. Not only was Naboth killed this way, but Jezebel had all his sons killed so that there would be no one to inherit the land she wanted to give to her husband as a gift. Ahab at least partially knew what happened—though perhaps not all the details. But when God gives you the authority to lead, he doesn't let you escape responsibility if you turn a blind eye to matters. King David went to great lengths to separate himself from the shedding of innocent blood that was done by those around him. By contrast, Ahab delightfully goes out to inspect his new garden while the dirt is still wet with Naboth's blood.

The King is strolling about the vineyard—celebrating the most futile of his misadventures to date—when Elijah appears. He sees the prophet and irritably greets him with the title of '*my enemy*'. Enemy? How many of us see the world like this? How often do we feel someone is our enemy because they tell us hard truths? Correction often feels like condemnation when we love our sin. Yet, there was no one else who prayed for Ahab's redemption like Elijah. Still, Ahab viewed him as an enemy. True friends do not always feel friendly. Our best friends will love us more than the fun of a relationship with us. They will risk our rejection in order to tell us what we need to hear.

Let's flip things around. Stand in Elijah's sandals a moment. How would you respond if someone labelled you an 'enemy' like Ahab did? What if you had been the one who firmly but lovingly spoke hard words to a friend—only to have them treat you like a foe? Most of us would find the experience painful. Our efforts are met with rejection. We get hurt, then angry. We either explode in their face or we quietly let our past concern and love for the person turn to bitterness. Our friend treats us like an enemy when we are trying to be helpful—so we react by treating them like an enemy in return. After lust, the most common character issue men report struggling with is anger.

Elijah doesn't do this. He doesn't call Ahab an 'enemy' back. He doesn't get verbal revenge. He doesn't yell, '*Do you know how much I've prayed for you?! Can't you see that I've only been trying to help you break free from the influence of that crazy she-demon of a wife that you're married to?! I'm your true friend—not her—yet you still treat me like rubbish!*' No, Elijah doesn't lose his temper out of self-pity or feelings of personal injustice.

But he doesn't back off either. Our culture often talks about the sin of *giving* offence. But Elijah knows that the sin here is one of *taking* offence (a common, but rarely talked about, sin in our generation). Elijah knows Ahab finds his words offensive. But he doesn't say '*Enemy?! What? Did what I say hurt your feelings? I am soooooo sorry. Tell you what, let's drop the whole thing and go grab a pint of lite beer.*' No, Elijah wouldn't say that.

Elijah doesn't drink lite beer.

Elijah is neither personally bitter at the unjust way Ahab has treated him, nor does he cower at Ahab's indignant reaction. He doesn't lose his cool. He calmly and faithfully pronounces God's word to him—words that are hard to say and hard to hear. They are words about sin, judgement, and demise. These are gospel words. They let men know that *'the wages of sin are death.'* Elijah is a faithful friend—though Ahab does not acknowledge him as such. He is not controlled by Ahab's rejection. Ahab does not have the power to make Elijah stop caring for him or honouring him as King.

This works for those of us who speak to a wider audience through preaching or writing. In the 1950's, at the height of McCarthyism, it was the term 'communist' that was used to ruin someone's reputation—even with little or no evidence. Today that word has been replaced. 'Xenophobe', 'racist', and 'homophobe' are the pejoratives they now ejaculate at you in their arrogant hysteria. Those who do not know us well may hurl these verbal grenades because they see us like Ahab saw Elijah: as the enemy. This gives us the opportunity to grow in love by responding with blessing to those who curse us. We don't respond to haters in kind.

The fact that someone treats us as an enemy does not mean we need to respond to them in either fear or aggression. Someone's hatred of us does not define us. God's love does. People might get angry at us, but we know that this is never our goal. We are not those who get a kick out of working people up. Success is not making lost people angry. There are lots of egotistical and rude ways we could do that. Success is making hell angry.

Elijah gives the hard word. Though Ahab was not technically guilty in the modern, legal sense of the murder of Naboth, he was responsible before God. Elijah does not let him hide behind his wife's guilt as Adam sought to do with Eve. Elijah enunciates the divine sentence without dilution. It is prophecy with testosterone. And it works—at least to a degree. Ahab responds with a measure of humility that we have not seen before, not even at Carmel.

Amazingly, Ahab's repentance is enough for God to extend mercy and withhold judgement for a generation. Elijah didn't give up being loving and faithful in his exhortations, prayers, and rebukes towards Ahab and in the end, it bore fruit. This is the challenge for us: refusing to see even the most treacherous flesh and blood as our ultimate enemy, but always as an object of possible redemption.

Does Elijah Win?

'When Ahab heard Elijah's words, he tore his clothes, and put on sackcloth, and fasted. The word of the Lord came to Elijah, 'See how Ahab humbles himself before me? I won't bring evil in his days: but in the days of his sons.' -1Kg 21

What is 'success' for a prophet? How can we even begin to measure 'success' when it comes to serving God? Is a prophet successful if he gets stoned to death and then four generations later society builds a statue of him out of those same stones? Perhaps that's part of it. But there is more.

Elijah fought in prayer and speech for the heart of his King and his nation. If we see that as his goal, then we could argue that he was successful—at least to a small degree. God granted an epic-sized miracle at Mt. Carmel that resulted in the repentance of many in the nation. The monopoly of Baal and Asherah worship was weakened if not broken. And now we see that even Ahab has a period of humbling—to which God is willing to grant mercy and hold back his wrath for a season.

Other may argue that Elijah is not successful—not ultimately at least. Ahab's repentance hardly results in any spiritual growth or godly maturity in the years following. His son, who took the throne, was just as wicked as he ever was. And the nation eventually slid back into idol worship and sin, resulting in all Israel being destroyed or taken captive by the Assyrians 120 years later. If the nation was eventually destroyed doesn't it make all temporary successes irrelevant? Did Elijah merely slow down the inevitable march of God's retributive judgement?

At some point in our efforts to proclaim the name of our God, we have to ask what success looks like. What are we working for? What is the goal of all our labours?

Some say that success is obedience. This may be true—even profoundly so. After all, on the Last Day we will be told *'well done'* for being *'good and faithful'*. But though this answer is rich in one sense, it also pushes the question back so that we are then left asking: what *does* it look like to be faithful and obedient disciples in midst of a dark generation? What does a life of obedience look like?

Part of the obedience that shapes our understanding of success must include our praying and stewarding of the knowledge of God. We are not responsible for reaching past generations. Nor are we responsible for the actions of future generations—though we are responsible for handing on the baton of faith by training them well. What we, as the church, are responsible for is proclaiming a gospel of repentance and forgiveness to our generation. In his generation, Elijah won hearts. He left Elisha and the school of the prophets. We cannot guarantee that our grandchildren will choose to serve God, but we can leave a legacy big enough for them to be influenced. If we have talents from God, we are called to steward them for his glory in our world. Rusty and rarely used resources and talents will only cry out against us when the Judge walks through history's door.

No generation washes up onto the shores of this planet with a full theology of God and His salvation. It does not matter if the UK or USA once had a strong gospel light. Every generation needs to be re-evangelised. We cannot live on the repentance of our grandparents. The apostle Paul wrote, *'I am a debtor to both civilised and barbarians...so I am eager to preach the Good News.'* Do we feel this debt in prayer? Not all of us are public preachers. Not all of us write or blog. But all of us can have conversations with those in the world around us—and they are often the most powerful forms of witness.

The book of Kings tells us that Elijah successfully eases the floodwalls of judgement and unleashes the floodwalls of revival and reform. The book of our generation is still being written—and the role that your prayers, words, and actions play in it is yet to be seen.

A Contrary Word

'But I hate him. He doesn't ever prophecy anything nice. Just bad stuff.' -1Kg 22

We enter in on a state visit. King Ahab of Israel and King Jehoshaphat of Judah sit side by side on the threshing floor in Israel's capital of Samaria. It may be unwise company for the righteous Jehoshaphat to keep, but this episode is the beginning of the end for Ahab.

In Scripture, threshing floors are often symbolic places where characters are weighed and destinies determined. John the Baptist preaches about a threshing floor. He says in his sermon at the Jordan that Christ will arrive with a winnowing fork. If you are a city boy like me, this may require a bit of explanation. At the threshing floor, the good wheat is separated from worthless elements like husk and straw. When the Christ that John preaches shows up with a winnowing fork, the threshing has already been done. The expectant Christ then winnows. He takes the two groups to their separate destinations, thus finalising the process that's already begun.

What separated—or 'threshed'—the two groups was John's cry to repent. It was on the threshing floor of John's message where men's destinies were determined. *'The Pharisees and experts of the law had rejected God's will for them by not being baptised by John.'* They were winnowed by the word that John preached and found to be waste elements. They chose to justify themselves instead of repent. And it is on a threshing floor where one of our two Kings is about to be winnowed.

King Ahab had some military victories and is feeling confident. The presence of a political ally by his side adds to his sense of strength. He asks if Judah's King will join him in retaking some towns from Syria. Jehoshaphat foolishly agrees but wisely asks if strategic counsel can be obtained from one of Yahweh's prophets. Ahab agrees to his ally's request and formally gathers 400 clergy—all of whom start prophesying victory in the name of Yahweh.

It is worth asking where this serpentine synod comes from. At Mt. Carmel, 450 prophets of Baal and 400 prophets of Asherah gathered against Elijah. After the miracle of fire and the repentance that followed, it is recorded that they slew Baal's vile vicars, but it says nothing about those of Asherah. Some assume that they were slaughtered too. But could these 400 fake priests simply have changed their uniforms and continued their careers under a new name?

They may have *Yahweh* written on their social media bio but *Asherah* is written on their hearts. This is how fake teaching gets into the church. Ideas that are trendy and carry force in society come in through gifted teachers whose hearts are not submitted to the full counsel of God's word. They coat godless ideas with Biblical language to make them palatable to Christians. Suddenly, young Christians think they are discovering in Scripture things that their spiritual forefathers have missed for 2,000 years. They see the Scripture with new eyes and are able to understand what all previous generations of Christians have missed for so long. *How clever we are!*

Or so we are led to believe. The preachers speak in Yahweh's name, but they do not speak the truth. But no one cares. They're prophesying victory against Syria for the King. This worship service is lit. The whole threshing floor is jamming. People are feeling spiritually high and good about themselves. Feedback is high on the swank-o-meter.

Isn't that the whole point of going to church?

But King Jehoshaphat isn't impressed. He understands that these guys are not the genuine article. He asks Ahab if there is a *real* prophet of Yahweh in the house and Ahab seems to reluctantly get his point. He concedes that if Judah's King really wants one of those old-school Yahweh preachers then, yes, there is one nearby. *'But I hate him. He doesn't ever prophecy anything nice. Just bad stuff.'*

Jehoshaphat insists on hearing from him. Predictably, the prophet Micaiah shows up and throws a damper on the whole sanctimonious affair. We'll talk more about him in a minute. For now, let us look at Ahab. It is how this King reacts to the prophet's word that determines his destiny.

Ahab doesn't listen. He has Micaiah removed for his 'hateful' words. And this is where we are today. We are a generation of Ahabs when it comes to the hard, direct bits of God's word. We don't like to be told that there are parts of our cultural values that God hates. If we are not openly hostile to these terribly untrendy sections of Scripture, then we are at least embarrassed by them and avoid them at all costs.

So, we do what Ahab did. We get rid of our Micaia and we keep the hip ministers that affirm us just as we are. We confine the not-so-nice prophets to prison by mocking, blocking, or excluding them through social media and other means. But it is ourselves that we've cut off by playing fast and loose with Yahweh's word. When we judge Scripture, it is we who are sentenced. It's our own damned destiny we confirm.

Say to the Seers: Do not see.

Say to the Prophets: Do not prophesy to us what is righteous.

Let us hear nothing more of the Holy One.

-Isaiah, 30.10

A Contrary Word II

'Let your word agree with theirs. Speak in a way that goes down well.' -1 Kg 22

To Micaiah's credit, he does wield irony with finesse and brandishes a cracking sense of humour as he speaks God's word to Ahab and the others at the threshing floor. But his message runs counter to the popular sound bites of the day. Micaiah is even told upon entering the synod that—for the sake of spiritual unity—he should say the same things the other preachers are saying. And so he does. He does with sarcasm dripping from his mouth like gravy.

The pressure on preachers and Christians in every generation to be unfaithful to God's word is immense. The early church was pressured to burn incense to Caesar. Protestants in 16th Century Europe were pressured by Catholic authorities to not publish the Scriptures in the language of the people. 18th and 19th Century Christians were pressured to compromise their beliefs with Deism and an anti-supernatural view of the Universe.

Our generation has its own pressure points of compromise. Micaiah had his. All he had to do was say that his King would be victorious in battle over the Syrians. He simply had to agree with all the other 'Yahweh' prophets. *Isn't that the humble thing to do? After all, who's to say that they were wrong and he was right? Why say things that some would deem hateful?* Insecurities can be all over the place when it comes to our witness.

Sarcasm & Wit

There is nothing wrong with using humour or sarcasm to make a point in our sermons, blogging, or witnessing if it is employed under the right conditions. Micaiah brilliantly says the exact opposite of what is expected. He shouts, *'March forward and succeed!'* thus getting behind Ahab's adverse attitude and towards him. The fact that he says something in agreement with the other faux-preachers is so shocking (or Micaiah's tone was so obviously facetious) that the King finds himself shouting, *'Tell me the truth in the name of Yahweh!'* When the prophet then speaks the blunt truth of his coming death, the impact must have been powerful to everyone listening.

Elijah also displayed similar wit in his encounter with the fake prophets on Carmel. *'So where is Baal? Is out grabbing a caramel latte?'* Jesus does similar things in his encounters with the Pharisees and Sadducees before his death.

In all these cases, the prophets are not speaking to God's faithful people. Nor are they speaking to lost and ignorant pagans generally. They are speaking to contrary crowds. Micaiah speaks to fake teachers and apostates who have the Scriptures but who reject them for their own ideas. He is not just speaking to blindness, but to wilful blindness and wit and humour can be clever tools in getting behind hostile defences and helping such people to see themselves.

It should also be noted that Micaiah and Elijah both use their sarcasm from a place of weakness. When we use sarcasm from a place of power, it can be distasteful and sound like the words of a bully. But when it's spoken in perilously weak situations, it can be glorious. It can diffuse some of the hostility and at least give you a hearing. Micaiah is standing alone, surrounded by enemy prophets and soldiers who won't hesitate to imprison or kill him. If you can wield sarcasm when looking down the barrel of a gun to the man you're speaking to, that's worlds away from using it to cyberbully someone. Speaking truth humorously to power is a sign of hope. The winsomeness of vulnerable saints can be a mighty offence to hell.

In fact, Micaiah shares first place with Ahab for the prize of the best one-liner in this section of Scripture. When punched by one of the fake preachers and asked, *'How did God's Spirit go from me and speak to you?'*, Micaiah replies, *'You'll see—when the day comes that you run and hid in a closet!'*

How do you top that? The prophets are a colourful bunch. They should be. Orthodoxy is the wildest.

Of Faithfulness and Trolls

Yes, we *should* try to make our witness accessible and able to be understood by those with little to no church background or theological understanding. It is good to speak the language of the people and know how to delightfully diffuse a contrary crowd when necessary. There's nothing wrong with trying to be seeker intelligible or sensitive in that sense. That is merely part of being a good missionary. But there is a doozy of a difference between adjusting the method, tone, or vocabulary we use to effectively deliver a message and actually adjusting the message itself. Lies will come into this world. For a season, they will triumph. But let them not come through us.

There are some people so desperate for attention that they will say the most outlandish things just to get it. That is not most preachers or even most Christians I know. Most Christians have no desire to get personally branded as a 'hater', 'bigot', 'homophobe', 'hate preacher', or—the ghastliest of all pejoratives—'a fundamentalist'. Only socially deficient people relish bad press in this way.

Micaiah is not one of these. He is not yelling outside the castle with rude signs. He is dragged in. But once the spotlight was on him, he faithfully and intelligently delivered God's word in protest to the dominant religious message of the moment. He knew it would cost him personally. He didn't want to go to prison. He may have had a wife and children at home. When we stand by ourselves and there are 400 voices opposing us, it is easy to feel insecure and alone. But a man who stands and speaks with God is always a majority.

To deliver the full counsel of God's word in any generation will cost us opportunities and friends. If you seek to be a reformer by carrying a contrary word to our generation—and if God gives you large influence—you will attract enemies. At first, they will ignore you. Then, when you begin to get traction and your influence grows, they will laugh at you. After that, when you don't cease and desist in the face of their mockery, they will come after you and vomit sewage at you to destroy you. The more of God's love and truth you seek to bring into the world, the more of man's hatred and deception you will have to wade through. But then? At the end? You will overcome and be seated victoriously with Christ.

And the world will be better for it.

We can only fulfil his call if we stay close to the cross. When we forget his acceptance, we become far needier for the smiles and 'likes' of those around us. But we've been given a book, marching orders, and a general that we report to who is worthy of all our love and loyalty. He will stand with us and support us when we feel alone in our witness. And in that moment, when everything visible seems against you, you may find yourself speaking the truth with a bold joy and sarcasm that baffles your enemies and opens some of their ears.

Shooting Ahab

'A man drew his bow, and struck the King of Israel.' -1Kg 22

Ahab has been subject to the influence of Jezebel for 20 years. All this has begun to grow a rather particular brand of cultured insanity inside of our King. Sin always corrupts our sanity. As we have already noted in the previous readings, the scene starts with him and Jehoshaphat in Samaria. Ahab wants this King of Judah and his forces to accompany him into battle against the punk King from Aram.

Micaiah has already told Ahab not to go into battle. This prophetic word makes Ahab uncomfortable enough to close his ears and harden his heart. Ahab has worshipped comfort, has indulged his own desires, and has become a slave to his own masturbatory choices. By rejecting Micaiah's word, Ahab turns away from any previous steps he may have made in repentance. It has now been years since the revival on Carmel and the more recent moment of prayerful humility that he experienced in Naboth's vineyard seems long gone. The royal dog may be returning to five-starred vomit, but it is vomit still.

Ahab refused to live a life of repentance as he let himself drift down the ever-flowing stream of human rebellion. Ahab becomes like his master. Because he did not lead his wicked wife into embracing truth, the queer Queen leads him into embracing manipulation. Ahab does something completely Jezebellic in the final moments of his life. He manages to convince Jehoshaphat to dress up like the King of Israel while he goes into the battle disguised as a regular soldier. How he managed to spin that one to Jehoshaphat, we do not know. We may imagine that he picked up a lot of tricks from Jezebel over the years. When we let ourselves be deceived, eventually we become deceivers. We are either becoming more a prophet of Yahweh or more a product of Jezebel every day of our lives.

But Ahab's sin has gone far enough. God steps in and brings the judgement on this man that he is overripe for. The wicked are usually surprised when judgement falls. The time God mercifully gives them to repent is mistaken for approval of their compromised lives.

Though disguised to avoid enemy attention, a stray arrow hits Ahab. The King bleeds to death in his chariot. Here is yet another antithesis between him and the prophet who continually spoke to warn and save him. While Elijah is taken up into the glory of eternal life in a chariot, Ahab dies in hellish shame in one.

The reflective contrasts between their lives were many. Elijah followed Yahweh. Ahab followed Baal. Elijah leads a school of prophets. Ahab commanded his wife's army of priests. Ahab was petulant. Elijah was consistent. Elijah prayed the widow's son to life, but pronounced death over Ahab's son. Elijah led a Phoenician woman into the light so that she could live. Ahab let himself be led by a Phoenician woman into the shadows. And in the shadows, he died.

In CS Lewis's powerful novel *'Till we have Faces'*, princess Psyche hears *'We must die before we die. There's no chance after.'* If Ahab had put to death his own sinful heart, his life would have gone differently. When we die to self, we begin to live to God. The invitation to come and die with Christ is not usually an attractive one. At least not at first. But when we keep our eye on the glory and life that comes through this dying, we can embrace the cross with joy.

God loved Ahab enough to send him the greatest prophet on the planet. But he chose to listen to the more polished, more educated, more beautiful voice of his wife. He inherited Israel in a state of spiritual dusk—and let it slide into the death throes of an irreversible gloom.

Elijah was the embodiment of those times. Those times were times of vengeance. The intercessor was not to be clothed with an olive branch with its fillet of wood, the symbol of a suppliant for mercy, but with fire, the symbol of justice and the messenger of wrath.

-EM Bounds

#ElijahMen

Is God Violent?

'O man of God, I plead with you, let my life, and the life of these fifty men, be precious in your sight. I know that fire came down from heaven, and burnt up the two captains and their squads of fifty men each.' -2Kg 1

King Ahaziah, son of the late King Ahab, sends a captain with 50 soldiers to fetch Elijah who is sitting on a hill. Like the King, this captain and his soldiers have no fear of God. They arrogantly command Elijah to obey the message like he is the King's lapdog. This is the same prophet who called down fire on Carmel. He is the one who predicted the death of this King's daddy. He prayed and held back rain clouds from Israel for three years. It would be sanity for the King to come and bow before Elijah and ask for his mercy. But he treats Elijah with contempt—and therefore he treats Elijah's God with contempt. As Jesus will say centuries later, whoever rejects you, rejects me.

Not only does the King display disdain towards God, but the first group of soldiers do as well. As a result, God rains fire down on all of them. The King then sends another fifty up the hill in an equally proud manner—and God napalms the lot of them too. Lastly, a third captain goes up in humility, falls on his knees, and asks for mercy. They live. But the King who witnessed these acts of judgment and mercy hardened his heart, did not repent, and died.

Liberal and unbelieving commentators don't like this passage. Sadly, their remarks insinuate that Elijah and God weren't acting very 'Christian'. Last century, Arthur Wallis—at the beginning of his landmark book, *God's Chosen Fast*—wrote, *'When people do not like the plain literal meaning of something in the Bible they are tempted to spiritualise it, and so rob of its potency.'* What was true of the church's reading of passages dealing with fasting in the 1960's, is true today of the church's reading of passages regarding God's violence. We are a generation that emphasises our understanding of God's love to the exclusion of many of his other attributes. (Thus, we have a culturally conditioned and confused idea of what His 'love' really is.)

129

When we look at passages where God sends physical judgement against men and women, we have a few ways to ignore them. The first is the way of unbelief. We simply chose to believe that this unsavoury portion of Scripture is not true, that it was accidentally included in the Bible, or that it is not inspired by God.

Another way is by allegorising. This method is simple enough to employ. We say that Joshua invading Canaan is about us violently fighting the sin in our lives or that Elijah calling down fire on wicked soldiers is about letting God judge sinful passions when they threaten to take control of our attitude. Of course, we can agree that some of these imaginative readings of the passage may have some useful application. Allegory is not always inappropriate in how we relate to Scripture. But it doesn't change the original story, does it? God still did these violent acts in real space and in real time.

Others say that every time God is angry or judges in the Bible that it is always restorative and never retributive in nature. One wonders how Korah, Sodom, Ananias, or Saphira were 'restored' when God struck them dead in their sin. A plain reading of many passages seemingly indicates that God often executes both restorative *and* retributive judgment—and that the two are not mutually exclusive. Often, in dispensing of retributive judgement on the wicked, God brings restorative judgement to the wider group.

A recent book by a well-known progressive leader tries to challenge the notion of a violent or 'warrior God' and proposes yet another way of dealing with judgement passages while attempting to hold to an Evangelical view of Scripture. He argues that God is allowing himself to be depicted in this violent way so that humanity can see just how violent they themselves are—and be repulsed. He argues that God's actions in the Old Testament are like the work of the cross in the new: *we are supposed to see it and be appalled at our own violent sinfulness*. If you're having trouble getting your head around this one, you are not alone. In addition to being confusing, the whole thesis presumes that these violent judgements by God are morally 'wrong'.

But there is a much easier way forward than by doing interpretive gymnastics. And that is by simply taking the Bible at face value—assuming that it actually means what it says. We take it like we take our shots: straight. If a person with no church background was given a Bible to read through, do any of us truly believe that she would then describe the God of the Bible as always being non-violent? Hardly.

The problem is not with the Bible. The problem is with us. 21ˢᵗ Century Westerners often have difficulty imagining a God who both violently punishes the wicked and who is also compassionate, and kind. But our difficulties in understanding are not the ultimate problem. Every culture has difficulty understanding at least some aspect of God's character. In the Middle East, it's the Trinity. In India, it's the exclusive nature of Christ. In honour bound cultures it's forgiveness. The problem comes when we exalt our cultural values above the Bible and begin to find clever ways of dismissing the bits that don't agree with us. Our attitude towards God's word reveals our true attitude towards God.

For some among us, the reason we hesitate to acknowledge God's violence is the notion that belief in a violent God will produce violent people. But this is not so. It is precisely because God will punish the wicked that I can be free from the need to do so. This is why Paul says, '*avenge not yourselves, but rather give place for God's wrath: for it is written, Vengeance is mine; I will repay, saith the Lord*'. Vengeance is His and that frees me to be a peaceful person.

One may say that we don't have the moral right to be violent towards others. Granted. But we are not God. God has the right to get aggressive in ways that we don't. He gives life, and He can take it back. The New Testament says that we are to '*behold both the kindness and severity of God.*' When we dismiss one at the expense of the other, we get in trouble. There should be times—though certainly not all the time—when the Bible is preached in a way that causes us to see God's severity. This creates in us the attitude demonstrated by the third Israeli captain who humbles himself before Elijah. We approach a God who punishes wicked people. We do not approach Him telling Him about how good we are, what rights we are entitled to, or how He *ought* to be kind to us. We acknowledge that we deserve the same flames that consumed the others—and we humbly run to the cross and ask for mercy. For it is at Golgotha where judgement and mercy meet. It's on that hill where God calls down fire on Himself—so that He won't have to call it down on us.

Elijah Men

'The sons of the prophets were at Bethel.' -2Kg 2

Elijah is getting ready to depart. He has fought the good fight and finished his race. By God's persevering grace, he is ending well. He is accompanied by his mentee and friend, Elisha. He will continue on Elijah's work and finish those parts of his mission that remain undone after he is gone. Elisha has been loyal, and loyalty in a mentee is not always a given. His faithfulness to his older friend and teacher will soon be rewarded.

We have also seen something about Elijah: his word is true. He told Ahab that it wouldn't rain by '*my word*', and it didn't. He told Obadiah that he would appear that very day before Ahab, and he did. Now he tells his protegee that if he sees him depart, he will get something of great value.

We live in a generation that is weak at keeping its word whenever it is inconvenient or costly to do so. We have divorce, friendivorce, broken contracts, claims culture, etc. As men of God, we must keep our word. We must keep it even when it hurts. Elijah lived this way, and now Elisha has no doubt that his mentor's words are fully reliable as they approach the end.

As Elijah travels, we see that he is leaving behind more than just Elisha. Throughout the journey they encounter pacts of zealous young men who are loyal to Elijah and eager to see Baal's influence broken in their nation. Like the eldest brother in a Hebrew family, Elisha will get a double spiritual portion of what these other disciples get. But it should be noted that Elijah is not just leaving behind this one exceptional mentee—he is leaving behind a rambunctious movement of holy young men.

These are the 'sons of the prophets'. The Hebrew word here is *ben* and it means 'son' in the widest possible sense—literal and figurative. This group gets its name by following the teachings of Elijah and other recognised prophets. They are Elijah Men. They refuse the influence of their queen. They are scallywags for Yahweh; men who seek to reform themselves and their nation. At least some of these men aspire to be prophetic voices. They can be thought of as a 'company' (NIV) or a 'school' of prophets. They are a movement against what Jezebel has created and are counterculturally turning Israel back to her God. Apostate generations need movements of reforming, prophetic voices. They need Elijah Men.

Jesus himself is our ultimate Prophet. He is the one who not only speaks God's words but who is God's word. We embrace the example of the prophets because all of them point us to Christ. This is why John writes in Revelation, '*The testimony of Jesus is the Spirit of prophecy*'. Walking in the footsteps of the prophets strengthens our loyalty to Jesus—it doesn't distract us from it.

It is urgent that in in the midst of apostasy we let the prophetic side of our Christian discipleship shine forth. When Peter stood up at Pentecost and preached a bold sermon that turned the hearts of thousands to repentance, he cited Joel's prophecy that '*your sons and daughters will prophesy*.' It is not the focus of this book to discuss all that is meant in Acts by '*the baptism of the Holy Spirit*', but one reoccurring feature of this apostolic phenomenon is clear: *and they spoke the word of God boldly*. Perhaps no other sign will be so evident of the Spirit's activity than that of men and women courageously speaking and writing gospel truth. Christ's people will declare his praises in godless environments. They will be fiercely loyal to Jesus. They will proclaim that the whole world should bow the knee to Christ—and that all other options are fakery.

Are we really sons of the prophets, or are we just play acting? Are we being discipled? Are we letting Holy Ghost filled men pour into our lives? Likewise, who are we discipling? If you were taken away by God, who would you leave behind to finish the work you have begun? Part of our success is handing the baton on to a successor. Is our church like a refrigerator—coolly preserving piety? Or, are we like an incubator that hatches out new converts and grows young disciples? Are we learning to walk in a counter-cultural holiness and calling others to do the same? In the midst of sinful insanity, the church cannot afford to be a mere club. We must be a prophetic movement.

It is our prayer that in the midst of apostasy and fake teaching, with so many visible leaders silent on pressing issues, that God would raise up a bold movement of nameless, faceless, unknown scallywags that would faithfully speak God's word in power, see the works of Jezebel torn down, and God's people built up. May God give us Elijah Men.

Chariots of Fire

'Elijah went up to heaven in a whirlwind.' -2Kg 2

Every life is full of days. But not all days are full of life. Ahab and Elijah both end their earthly lives in a chariot: one is a chariot of blood, the other of fire. It is an ending marked with shame for the first man. It is a moment of unparalleled glory for the second man. Elijah lived every day with eternity in view. Now he steps into that place where his heart has long resided.

There are three great moments in the life of every Christian. The first is the day of his birth. Over this moment he has no influence and is powerless to stop it. The second great moment is the day he meets his saviour. The third great moment is the day of his death. We may be powerless to stop the fact that we will die, but we are not powerless to influence how much glory will be in that moment.

For the secularist, there is no glory in death. If we take the material view, then the bio-machine that carries you around and gives you the illusions of consciousness, dignity, beauty, and love merely falters. The sad mystery that is organic ageing ends yet another one of those peculiar accidents that manifested themselves upon planet earth.

By contrast, the Christian will step into eternity knowing, that both by life and by death, he is the sole property of Jesus Christ. Whether the days of his life have been numerous or few, Christ is there at the end. He has been bought with his Master's blood and the grave does not hold final claim over him. He dies with confidence—not because he thinks that he has been a great Christian—but because he knows that Jesus is a great Saviour.

I do not fully understand how rewards in Eternity work. But Jesus speaks of them. Since eternal life is a gift from Christ, many of us are hesitant to focus on rewards. And yet we must. Scripture demands it. Eternity will be an unspeakable joy for all of God's hallowed people, but somehow there are things we can do to enrich that.

Jesus commands us to store up riches in heaven. Somehow the sacrifices we make for the name of Christ in this life will greet us a hundred-fold on the other side. Jesus commanded us to use our worldly resources so that eternal friends would be there to greet us in greater number on that final day. Heaven will be great for all. Our Creator will be there and we will see His face. But we are also guaranteed that we will never regret the sacrifices we made here on Earth of in order to give, fast, pray, and witnesses for Christ. Jesus is not only a great Saviour, he is also a great Rewarder. That is why we must consider Eternity's chariots. They are more real than anything else in our lives. Those eternal hooves are more solid than the paperback or kindle in your hands now.

A solid vision of eternity changes how we live here on earth—giving us far more strength to serve God, bless others, rebuke fake teachers, and glorify God. Let's illustrate this. Imagine a friend asks you to do a job for eight hours. He says that if you do it, he will pay you £50 ($60) at the end of the day. You agree and get to work. But no so sooner had you started, then people come in and start making fun of you as you work, calling you rude names. A crack appears in the ceiling above you and it starts raining on you. Your tools break, making the job far more difficult than you thought.

What would you do? Most would leave. The £50 would not seem worth the abuse. But imagine you are promised £50 million for that eight hours. At the end of the day, you will have riches like never before. How would you then experience the difficulties? Very differently. You would be whistling as it rained on you. You would cheerfully wave as the people made fun of you. And the blisters you got from your hard work would be incomparable to the riches that await you at the end of the day.

That is our lives. That is our reward. Yet we so often forget it—and we are weaker in life's difficulties as a result.

Live for that final day. Ask God to print a vision of a chariot on your eyes. If you do, you will live differently. Tribulations that overwhelm others, will only feel to you as '*light affliction*' (Rm 8). Generosity will come easy, because what you give away is merely stuff that fades. You can endure short hunger pains when fasting, because you see the eternal difference it is making. Your ears can endure the mockery of others, because you are daily preparing your ears to hear '*Well done good and faithful servant*' from their Creator. Do not leave this life timidly. Rage against hell until your final day. Eternity will be your retirement.

135

Day of the Eunuchs

'They threw her down. And blood splattered on the wall.' -2Kg 9

Jezebel led the people of God astray with her idolatry, violence, and sexual immorality. That which godly men in a godly age are ashamed to think about, she made common practice. She unleashed a torrent of spiritual sewage for decades, and now the Almighty is calling her to account.

Elijah had prophesied to Ahab years earlier that dogs would one day devour Jezebel's flesh. Being chewed up by dogs may seem to us a rather ironic prognostication for the Bible's most blasphemous bitch. Yes, this would be bad even in our day. But in the Ancient Near East, it was worse than bad. It was an abomination. Dogs were unclean. They were wild—not pets. It would be akin to being eaten by rats. In any case, it had been a word that Jezebel probably imagined would come to nothing. But every true word of God comes to pass. And it is interesting that God's sovereignty had ordained for eunuchs to fulfil it. It is eunuchs who slaughter this royal harlot. One who manipulates and destroys by perverting sex, cannot work her charms over one for whom sex has no controlling hold.

Jesus speaks of eunuchs. He had been speaking to his disciples on the subject of marriage and divorce. He affirmed to them that marriage was to be between one man and one woman for one lifetime. The disciples questioned if it was not better—since divorce is forbidden—to remain single. Perhaps the disciples were being a little bit cheeky in asking this. After all, in that conservative, Jewish culture, everyone got married—so Jesus' reply must have shocked them.

> *"There are some eunuchs who are born so, there are some who are made eunuchs by others, and there are some eunuchs who have made themselves so—for the sake of the kingdom of heaven. He who can receive this, let him."* -Mt 19

Jesus lists three types of eunuchs. There is some debate about what is meant by the first—those eunuchs who are *'born so'*. We understand the second—some male slaves had their parts removed for service by powerful rulers. In neither of these cases is being a eunuch seen as desirable. But then Jesus mentions a third type of eunuch. A voluntary one.

No, it doesn't involve getting a knife and doing extreme surgery on yourself. Jesus is speaking of those who will live celibate lives for his glory. These are people who will show the world that sex is not their ultimate treasure. This is not the spiritual gift a lot of young people are eager to get. *'Not all can receive it'* the Master says.

Some of these may be people who have SSA (same-sex attraction) and no opposite-sex attraction. In popular speak, we would say they are gay without any hints of heterosexual attraction ever sneaking in. They forgo satisfying sexual urges out of obedience to Christ and they do not pursue marriage with someone of the opposite gender. Some of the UK's most powerfully used Christian leaders fit this description. But it doesn't have to be someone with SSA. Some may simply choose—regardless of sexual desires—to lay marriage aside to better serve God.

Those who voluntarily embrace celibacy are an offence to Jezebel. Part of her power lies in sexual trickery. But there are those who will not be controlled by that. Jezebel misleads because she teaches people to equate intimacy with sex. But whereas we all need love and intimacy to prosper, we do not need sex to do so.

Those who voluntarily choose to live celibate lives for the sake of Christ, have a special authority to confront the sexually immoral teachings and behaviours of our day. Yes, all the pure in heart—married or unmarried—will have a degree of authority to confront her. But especially them. They are the ones who throw her down from the tower to the hungry dogs below. Twenty-four hours later, all that will be left of Jezebel is little piles of dog poo. A tribute to the wages of the sin and the victory of the eunuchs.

Should we Fear God?

'Don't fear those who kill the body but are not able to kill the soul; rather, fear Him who is able to destroy both soul and body in hell.' -Mt 10

In looking at Elijah's life it is impossible to escape the subject of the fear of the Lord. This attitude—one that Elijah embodies—is the outstanding enigma to much of Western Christian culture as we plod on into the 21st century. It is a subject of teaching largely ignored by many of our spiritual *pezzonovantes* in their blogs, videos, and bestselling books. Revelations of God's holiness causes one to tremble—and trembling is messy with a caramel macchiato in hand.

What exactly is the fear of the Lord? I hardly know. At least I know when it is, and when it is not, on my soul. It is not nightmarish. Demonic fear is confusing and paralysing. Godly fear is sobering and liberating. It helps one avoid sin—thus the Psalmist says about the wicked *'there is no dread of God before their eyes.'*

To fear Him is to be in awe of Him. We fear God not because He is cruel and evil but rather because He is good and holy. Fearing Him causes us to run to the cross to find His limitless mercy when we sin. The fear of the Lord is what separates the pray-ers from the players. It is standing in the place of holy fire but not being consumed. It is the pathway to death-to-self and, therefore, enables us to stand in the power of resurrection life. It is the true confidence: fearing God more results in fearing men less.

Do we fear God? Not, *Do we think God is hip?* Nor *Do we have a popular ministry of writing, preaching, dancing or singing?* There is perhaps no more accurate measuring stick of one's greatness in God or of one's potential for bearing eternal fruit than this one quality which is almost impossible to overvalue. This is the heart of Elijah. He was able to stand boldly before Ahab in public because he bowed low before God in private. And Jesus—our new and better Elijah—is said to have *'delighted himself in the fear of the Lord'*.

What gave the Hebrew women courage and strength to defy the Pharaoh and save babies in ancient Egypt? Scripture declares it is because they *'feared God'* (Ex 1). What gave Paul the power to keep persuading hostile crowds to consider Christ while facing obstacles of elephantine proportions in city after city? '*Therefore knowing the fear of the Lord, we persuade people.*' (2 Cor. 5)

One will not know true and lasting closeness to God without it. It was central to Jesus' relationship to the Father, '*His delight will be in the fear of the Lord*' (Isaiah 11). The Fear of the Lord is '*The beginning of wisdom*' (Pr. 1) and no one is a true theologian without it—regardless of how many degrees one has on the wall or what academic journals one gets published in.

It is also through Jesus that we can experience God and not be consumed. He satisfied divine wrath by paying the price for human sin. Apart from Jesus, God is dangerous. Christ is the secure asbestos suit we put on if we are to safely enter the volcano of God's presence. In him, we are safe. The fire becomes fatherly. But still, falling into the hands of a fire is fearful—even if he is *Abba*.

Preacher, what is the effect of your ministry upon those you speak to? Are we merely entertaining or boosting self-esteem? Or, do people leave our services humbled and speechless because they have had a revelation of the awesome majesty of God? Christian, are we bored of prayer? Are we constantly distracted by other thoughts in times of public worship? Or, does the Fear of God rest on us to such a degree that we hunger to engage with God in private because nothing else is as satisfying to us? In all our getting, may we get this. Too much is at stake in our generation to go without.

Stand firm in the faith.

Act like men.

Be strong.

-Paul, 1 Corinthians 16

#ElijahMen

Elijah, Malachi & the New Ahabs

'I am going to send Elijah before the awesome day of Yahweh.'-Mal 4

Four hundred years after Elijah and just as many before John the Baptist, we have Malachi. His name means 'messenger'. He is a messenger and part of his message is about another messenger.

Like in the New Testament epistle of James, we can hear the voice of Elijah in this short book of Malachi. This is because what we see in Elijah, Ahab, and Jezebel is more than just a great story. This battle continues to repeat itself among the people of God throughout the generations. Elijah and Ahab are not just something that happened. They are always happening. We can see these dynamics both repeatedly at play both in Scripture and in church history.

Like Elijah, Malachi comes onto the scene without fanfare or warning. Like Elijah, he calls God's people away from spiritual and sexual compromise and back to holiness for his generation has seen a Jezebellic spectre at work in the nation, polluting both worship and marital fidelity. Like Elijah, his words are few, but they pull no punches. His vocabulary makes most of our British pulpiteering look tame and overly modest by comparison.

But unlike Elijah, Malachi doesn't speak to one particular man. There is no King at this time. Rather, he speaks to a whole generation of Ahabs. There is no singular Jezebel leading them astray. The spirit of this world has slowly seduced the hearts of God's men and left them spiritually impotent.

Unlike Elijah, Malachi is not up against the fake prophets of Baal and Asherah. He is now speaking out against the priests of Yahweh. Though outwardly they appear to be representing God, the spiritual food they feed His people and the examples they set are both an abomination to the Holy One of Israel. Unlike Elijah, he does not slaughter them with the sword. But he sets the sharp prophetic word he's been entrusted with against them in order to split spirit and soul asunder.

141

Malachi reminds us that Jezebel may often come in more subtle packaging and we may be in the midst of God's people yet have hearts like Ahab without realising it. We may still attend church, sing songs, and give some money. But in spite of all these religious trappings, our hearts do not burn with God's fire. We may not be worshipping idols with prostitutes, but we may be singing God's praises with our lips while our eyes caress the body of another man's wife. And it takes a prophet like Malachi to wake us up to our condition.

Malachi reminds us to be careful when we pray for revival. He asks, '*But who can stand the day of his appearing? For he shall come as a refiner's fire.*' Most of us would like things to pick up a bit in our local congregations. We'd like a bit more buzz around our churches and chapels with a few new visitors coming through. But do we really want true Holy Ghost revival? Do we want the God of Holiness to come into our midst and shine his spotlight on us? Only by greatly humbling ourselves will we be able to live with such true, continual burning. The flames of heaven are much hotter than those of hell at times.

On the final pages of the Hebrew Scriptures, God reminds us of Elijah. Not only does Malachi carry this prophet's message of wholehearted loyalty to Yahweh, but he also prophesies another Elijah. This one will come to introduce the Messiah. He will turn the hearts of the fathers to the children—and how our world needs spiritual fathers!

In this sense, Elijah is the bridge between the two Testaments. After rebuking Jezebel's influence in his nation, Malachi finishes with a prophecy about Elijah's reappearing. We are not far into Matthew's gospel before we see Elijah's prophetic ministry once again rise up out of the desert sands of time.

The Topless Prophet: part one

'In those days John came preaching in the wilderness.' -Matt 3

'John, keep your head on!'

That's what the pundits started saying when he spoke against the sexual sin of those in power. *'It's contrary to God's law for you to marry your brother's wife!'*, the prophet firmly proclaimed.

His friends are probably telling him to tone it down a bit. But John is an Elijah Man. In fact, he is the uniquely prophesied Elijah Man talked about by Malachi 400 years earlier. And his prophetic rebuke rings out over the swirling desert sands, disturbing the comfort of everyone who had become laid back and tolerant over such matters.

From our sophisticated, 21st Century, Western perspective, we wonder if John couldn't be just a bit nicer. After all, it is being said that when our dear queen first heard John's cruel words, she went back to her castle to cry, indulge in chocolate ice cream, and garner social media sympathy points. *'That John is such a hater!'* She tweets as she lambasts the preacher's *'toxic masculinity'*.

The poor cupcake. She is, after all, just a desperate castlewife. Preachers aren't supposed to say things that offend rich, powerful, and sexually immoral women. Are they?

When hearing statements that cut across our comfort levels, we should ask, *Is this true?* John's rebuke against Herod's sexual sin is based on a law in Leviticus. It is stated in chapters 18 and 20. And though Scripture directs us to usually give rebukes in private, Herod was a public figure sinning publicly and unapologetically—therefore a public rebuke was appropriate. It is the same today. (1 Tim 5.20)

Is the Bible Understandable?

Have you ever worked with children? One of the things mine do, when I ask them about something they're uncomfortable with, is to pretend they don't understand what I'm saying.

Me: *Did you clean your room like I asked you to?*
Child: *Room? Which room? Our house has lots of rooms.*

Or

Me: *Did you hit your little brother?*
Child: *Brother?*
Me: *Yes, your little brother. The one who is six.*
Child: *What do you mean by 'hit'?*

We are big children and we do this with the words of our Heavenly Father when he says things in Scripture that we are not comfortable with. Here in the 21st Century Anglo-Saxon world, we have become masters of this art. If John lived in our day and issued his rebuke, the crowd around him would give him feedback along these lines:

John: *It is not lawful for you to marry or sleep with your brother's wife!*
Us: *John, are you sure that's relevant? There are far worse sins happening.*
Us: *Moses is no longer the ruler of Israel John, we're in Greco-Roman times now. We know things the ancients didn't.*
Us: *Sheep and the Goats John—at least Herod feeds the poor. That's what counts.*
Us: *Don't judge John. Focus on your own sin.*
Us: *But John, that rule is taken from Leviticus—and that book has some weird stuff in it.*
Us: *John, you should stick with your message about sharing our clothing with the needy. That bit went down well in the media.*
Us: *But God is love, and if Herod and Herodias really love each other, why would you want to keep them apart?*
Us: *Moses wrote that in Hebrew 1,500 years ago. We speak Aramaic. You need to understand the word for 'brother' meant something different in the original dialect.*

Clarity

When the serpent got Eve to sin, he first fed her the idea that God's Word was vague and confusing. *'Did God really say…?'* he whispered. By contrast, God's people are at their strongest when they reflect on Scripture and say things like: *'The unfolding of your words gives light; it gives understanding to the simple.'* (Ps 119).

144

It is blasphemy to excuse our laziness in the study of Scripture by blaming God for not being clear enough on an issue.

Yes, there are some issues that the Bible does not address and we are either ignorant or uncertain in these matters. There are things we may wish the Bible did clearly address, but it doesn't. The Bible may direct you to care for your body, but it won't tell you exactly what diet or exercise program to embrace. It is wrong to assume it speaks on things it does not—and thus add to the Word of God. But it is equally wrong to take from Scripture by feigning an uncertainty that careful study will show is unwarranted. Finding solid, relevant answers usually does not require formal theological education. At best, the training involved in getting a theology or Bible degree may help us explain why some of the new, creative, and contortionist interpretations—the ones that get the passages to say something other than what they obviously mean—are in error. Deception relies on confusion. But John takes his Bible like we should take our whisky. Straight.

The Topless Prophet: part two

Herodias is livid. The scandalmongers are chatting away about her improper sex life and they are not just tossing twaddle. The desert preacher accurately rebuked her husband in public over ditching his previous wife for her and now the elite gossips are talking about her as if she was a political whore.

Which she is. She just doesn't fancy being thought of as one.

She is angry and lays plans to manipulate her husband, into getting what she wants. She has her hot daughter do a striptease before the drunk ruler and his buddies. Like most men in such situations, he just sits and stares like a dumbassador from the Republic of Stupid. With Herod's brain half dead on lust over his step-daughter, Herodias gets him to order John's execution and the Baptist goes topless in the worst possible way. If John is an Elijah man, Herodias is certainly a daughter of Jezebel.

We might then hear the pundits of the day commenting, *'If only John had stuck to that nice, charitable "share what you have" sermon and left people's sex lives alone, he might've been ok. Why did have to go a start protesting against sexual immorality?'* We might ask a similar question about the church today: Is speaking out on sexual sin central to our mission? Are adultery, fornication, homosexual acts, and pornography small issues that we should just sweep under the rug, keep for closed room conversations, or agree to disagree on?

Some are now saying, 'yes'. They argue that people need a new heart more than a new sex life. They rightly point out that huge amounts of social and political controversy have circled marriage and sex related issues over the last couple of decades. *'Surely'* they say, *'wading into these waters will only distract from the simple message of the cross and resurrection of Jesus. And we want to be known for what we're for rather than what we're against. Right?'*

The reasoning is coherent. We do not want to distract from the Gospel. And yet, we must then ask, *'what is our gospel?'* Jesus says in Luke that the Gospel is one of *'repentance and forgiveness of sins.'* If that is the case, we must ask what exactly it is we are to call people to repent of and seek forgiveness for?'

And this is where prophets get into holy trouble. They stop speaking in milquetoast platitudes. Prophets have backbones made of something other than sweet pastry. They specific about sin. John gave out specific advice to specific people about what they needed to repent of. There was no, 'everyone try to be less selfish and grumpy' type preaching.

John told the soldiers to repent of abusing their authority. He told the rich to share and told the non-rich to be content with their wages (leaving both capitalist and socialist feeling stung). And to the ruler who was living openly and unrepentantly in the tolerated sexual sin of his day? 'Yes, you too must repent sir—of your sexual sin in particular.'

The early church preached a confrontational message to its surrounding culture. What was one of the chief social sins of the day? It was Emperor worship. People were allowed to worship other gods, as long as they also burned incense to Caesar and say, 'Caesar is Lord'. But the early church protested this. Their message was 'Jesus is Lord'. Now Jesus was also preached as Lord when the gospel spread outside of the Roman Empire and he is still preached as Lord now that the reign of the Caesars has ended. The early Christians did not invent theology just for the sake of being difficult. The gospel isn't anti-Empire any more than it is pro-Empire in that political sense.

In the context of Roman culture, the Lordship of Caesar was an idol that was particularly opposed to the gospel. The apostles knew that if repentance were to be real in their context, they must confront that idol. Yes, there were other cultural idols as well. The other big damnables of Roman culture were greed and sexual immorality—and they are also addressed in the apostles' letters.

And what are the big cultural idols of our day? We have more than one. Money is certainly up there. Politics too. But they are not alone. The idol of unfettered orgasm drives us as well. The perceived right to have sex with who I want and when I want—as long as it is consensual—is taken for granted.

John's Gospel (the other John) tells us that 'Light has come into the world, but people loved darkness instead of light'. When light shines down on that which is shameful in our culture, we hate it, and do all we can to argue and reason against it. This is why Herodias wielded all her manipulative trickery with Herod—even to the point of pimping out her own daughter. She hated the light John was shining her way.

The result of John's preaching was his death. But very few sermons on Sunday in our day ever get near the point of being dangerous. Why? Is our culture less wicked than that of the Romans? Have we found a nicer way to present the gospel than John and the martyred apostles?

When preaching gets specific, things get intense. People get butthurt, and prophets lose their heads.

John's Dark Night

'Are you the one?'-Mt 11

Earlier we talked about Elijah's disillusionment when he scarpered off to Mount Horeb. John had a similar experience and it is worth exploring because many of us men will or have experienced what the forerunner did. Elijah's depression was a cocktail of negative emotions that at least included loneliness and intimidation. John's cocktail seemed to be a mixture of confusion and disappointment about how God was operating.

The accounts in the gospels are clear enough. Herod tosses John in jail for preaching against his sin with Herodias. John is spiritually strong enough to handle a few prison bars. But as time passes by, he keeps hearing reports about Jesus—and those reports do not match up with what John expects. He is confused—so he sends messengers to Jesus to ask if he really is the Messiah. Considering that John had baptised Jesus and already pronounced him as the Lamb of God, this is quite an emotive backpedalling from his earlier profession.

We do not know for sure what exactly John is expecting, but we can make reasonable guesses based on the summaries of John's sermons. It may be that John assumes the Messiah is going to have more of a ministry of visible judgement. It could be that he doesn't understand why Jesus is always eating and at dinner parties while he and his crew are fasting. He may wonder why this Messiah is letting him rot in prison instead of freeing him. *Why am I still in prison Lord? Couldn't I serve you better if I could get out and preach some more? How are these bars helping your cause?*

Sometimes we get offended by how God operates. When such things happen, inevitably there will arise bogus blenders who mix together modern pop-psychology and cheesy evangelical pietism. The results are phrases that are often as blasphemous as they are trite (perhaps that's oxymoronic - most blasphemy is trite). One of the most common of these phrases is *You just need to forgive God.*

149

This is not what Jesus says to John. The Son of God doesn't ask John to forgive him for not meeting his expectations. Instead, he responds to John's messengers by citing the Scriptures in connection with the miracles he is doing and then gives them a clear word to pass to John: *blessed are those who are not offended by me.*

He doesn't ask John's forgiveness for offending him. He says John will be blessed if he works through his unmet expectations and accepts who God is and what He's doing. King Jesus is not doing anything wrong by not doing what his servant expects. Jesus does not need forgiveness. He never has and never will.

It does not seem like Jesus says this in a harsh way. Jesus loves John. Jesus speaks these words in gentleness to a man who had spent years in prayer and fasting, drawing near to the God of Scripture. But John still had things to learn and unlearn (we all do). Disillusionment can be painful. But we must be disillusioned. We must have our fake theologies and expectations stripped from us if we are to grow. In the midst of ministry and fighting spiritual battles, such disillusionment is often unexpected and painful.

God allows disappointment, rejection, and betrayal to come into the lives of His men. Learning how to navigate and worship in the midst of these is part of the school we enrolled ourselves in when we began to follow Christ. We will not fulfil all our destiny as long as we allow ourselves to remain crippled by these wounds.

How do we work through our tendency to be offended? In such seasons, we learn to rest in our knowledge of God's goodness. We may not always be able to trace his hand, but we can trust His heart. And it is such trust that John must now embrace if his heart his to be free from offence.

Play the man, Master Ridley; we shall this day light such a candle, by God's grace, in England, as I trust shall never be put out.

-Hugh Latimer, to his friend Nicholas Ridley, as they were both about to be burned alive for their teachings and beliefs outside Balliol College, Oxford (16 October 1555)

#ElijahMen

I, Herod.

Dear 21st Century Christian M*en*,

I am Herod. My friends call me Antipas. I am not the Herod you hear about at Christmas—the one who slaughtered all the babies at Bethlehem. That was Herod the Great, my father. I was only a teenager when that happened.

Life started out well for me. When I began my reign, I had favour with the powers in Rome and accomplished some successful building projects near the Sea of Tiberias—or *Galilee* if you prefer the old, parochial speak. But despite these earlier successes, things did not end well. The marriage to my second wife, Herodias, added fuel to a border dispute I was having with King Aretas and a war broke out. He was annoyed—among other reasons—over the starter marriage I had with his daughter. (I divorced her to marry Herodias, you see.)

I lost that war because the reinforcements from Rome, ones that I had been depending on, never showed up. Two years after that, my nephew accused me of treason to Emperor Caligula. I was sent into exile—to Gaul of all places! I was sent here with nothing but my wife.

There was a young preacher-man named John. A strange lad who lived in the desert and only ate insects and bee's sugar (when he wasn't fasting). He had a bold spirit and warned me against marrying Herodias. She had been the wife of my half-brother since a very young age. But I was the ruler and I desired her. So, I invited her to be my wife. She divorced him and came to me. Whether she ever wanted to be married to me *for me* (or just for my throne) I do not know. I certainly did not care too much back then. She looked amazing and she made me feel amazing.

But in order to be ruler over those fundamentalist, Jewish nutjobs, one is supposed to obey what Moses wrote about gender, marriage, and sexuality. But really, how are we supposed to adhere to that stuff in our modern day? That was over 1,000 years ago! We've progressed so much since then. Moses predated Aristotle and Plato. People thought crazy things back in Moses' day. If I really loved Herodias, why should a Mosaic law, written in primitive times, keep me from her?

But when I listened to John preach the first time, I was not so sure. He was 15 years younger than me, but spoke with such conviction. I did not know if he was a wacky kid out of the desert or if he really was a messenger from the God of Abraham. People were whispering that he was Elijah back from the dead. To be honest, I was shaken. I wondered, *What if John is right? What if I should deny my lusts instead of pursuing them? What if the love I have for Herodias is not meant to be followed? What if certain ideas that my sophisticated Greek and Roman education taught me are wrong?*

I took my uncertainties to my new wife. She reassured me that love could never be sin and that John was nothing more than *'a fundamentalist, misogynistic, hate preacher'* to use her vocabulary. She wanted me to have him executed for rebuking us publicly. But many people believed he was a prophet and I, though I didn't tell Herodias, was not 100% sure that he wasn't. Instead of executing him, I had him silenced by locking him up in prison for his hateful speech against us. Herodias was not thrilled that I let him live. But I thought she would respect my decision as ruler and be satisfied he was silenced.

Then there was my birthday party. It was a proper blokes party and there was plenty to drink on tap. All was going well—until Salome showed up in *that* outfit. *Who is Salome?* Salome is my wife's daughter—a teenager at the time—and she had inherited all of her mother's feminine appeal and charm. I had noticed her before, but had never touched her out of fear of my wife. But now she was in my man cave (willingly!) and she wanted to give me the birthday present of a striptease. With all that beer in me, what man could say no? She began to dance. And she… she was incredible. *It's ok, she's not my real daughter, just my stepdaughter. She's here because she wants to be—no one is forcing her!* I repeatedly told myself as she danced.

I was dizzy with lust. But I was not alone. There was not a man in the room who didn't have drool running down his beard. But the whole show was poison! And this is why I write to you. Herodias was playing me like a fool. She had sent her daughter in there, knowing I was a lusty man. She was furious that I had not killed John and she was using her daughter to get her way. During the dance, Salome got me to promise to give her whatever she asked for. I was in such a state of drunken ecstasy that I agreed. How could I deny such cleavage?! I swore before all my guests that I would give her whatever she asked for *just don't stop dancing like that!* Don't all men swear such things when they're under the influence of sex? Eros! Now there's a deity no man can tame.

Then, the dance ended. The music stopped. And she did what I had not expected. She asked for the head of the preacher on a platter. My conscience screamed the way a man's does after he realises the wages that his sin pays. *Surely there must be way out of this!* I looked around the room. All eyes were on me. What could I do? I may have been a pervert, but to be a ruler worth my salt, I had to at least be a man of my word. I could not break a promise. Not a public one anyway.

Somehow in that moment I was sober. I knew that John was a prophet. Certain. He was in a dungeon while I was in the best room in the castle. He was languishing while I was lusting. And my sin was now the judge and jury that would silence his powerful voice forever.

I regretted what I did as soon as I had done it. But regret is not repentance. A year or so later I had the chance to set another prophet free, but I didn't do any better towards him either. This one worked miracles. But he refused to even speak when he was brought before me. I was offended by his lack of respect so I mocked him and sent him back to Pilate who executed him. Some believe that prophet rose from the dead.

Now I have nothing but this house in southern Gaul and the woman who I married contrary to the Law. Had I submitted to John's baptism of repentance, if I had stayed with my first wife, how might my life now be different? Men, do not follow my example. I had it all. But sin took me further than I expected to go and made me pay prices I never expected to pay. Men, listen to the words of the prophet. The fires of lust may burn strong, but the fires of regret burn stronger still—and I have a gnashing of teeth that feels like it will never end.

-Herod

Porn: Jezebel's Stronghold

Herod's sin of lust that leads to the Baptist's decapitation serves as a good moment to address a relevant issue: pornography.

The internet has made pornography—once only a snare for those minority of men willing to go out and buy a magazine—a trap to us all. And not just the men. Increasingly women are getting caught up in it too. Pornography is a far greater weapon of destruction in the church than any gay activism could ever be. It has become Jezebel's stronghold, keeping back a generation of Christians from going forward in confidant spiritual growth and ministry.

Now let us never misunderstand: sex is a good gift. We do not think of the human body as bad. God made it. I am convinced that boobs are a sign that God loves us and wants us to be happy. Let us give thanks where thanksgiving is due. But pornography turns our natural sexual drive into a system of chemical terrorism. One minute we're going about our business in a state of healthy sanity. The next minute—when ignited by a low neckline, short skirt, or sensual advertisement—we are grabbed by a furious desire to pant over cushions of flesh that are forbidden to us. We run to porn, covet, and believe our soul will only be satiated by the god of orgasm. Like all sins, this evil is goodness deformed.

Here, we share just a few short tips that many men have found helpful in gaining victory in their own souls.

First of all, realise there is usually no silver bullet. Rarely is there just one thing you must do in order to never struggle with sexual lust again. Pornography addiction is—in part—the result of other deep needs not being met in healthy ways or deep wounds not being properly healed. As we grow spiritually and find God's affirmation, acceptance, and love, we will be less tempted to seek it out on a computer screen. Yes, unless you have SSA exclusively, then as a man you will always have an attraction to the female body. But increased health brings increased self-control. This includes times of prayer, reading, and even getting enough sleep and eating well.

Secondly, do not isolate yourself. Porn makes a man feel dirty and guilty. Like Adam, he hides in shame. The ensuing loneliness makes porn all the more attractive and addiction becomes a downward spiral. Have quality friendships with brothers you can talk openly with. Also, have healthy relationships with women. Male-female friendships can be controversial, and it does have pitfalls. But Scripture commands us to treat women as sisters. We discuss this in more detail in the book *Forbidden Friendships*, but for now we simply note that having healthy relationships with women can help serve as an emotional deterrent to objectifying them on a computer screen.

Next, consider dealing with masturbation as a root cause. Yes, we know the Bible does not specifically mention masturbation and some men have a huge and often unnecessary guilt complex over this issue. But as a pastor that has worked with men over the years on this issue, many have found that they could not overcome pornography without also eliminating masturbation. Some disagree, but it has definitely been the experience of many. Porn and masturbation play off each other. Eliminating the one will help you get rid of the other.

Lastly, do not give up. The first of Luther's 95 theses was that a Christian's whole life should be one of repentance. Some men (and women) fight this new drug for a season and then give up after failing many times. Don't. This may be a war we fight our whole lives—but our souls are worth fighting for. Never raise the white flag and surrender. Keep making whatever practical changes are necessary to remove yourself as far from temptation as you can get: turn the angle of your computer screen to face the door, pledge to a trusted friend that you will never take your smartphone into the bathroom, etc. You are in a war. If we seek to reform a compromised church, we must reform our compromised selves. Keep doing whatever is necessary to gain ever-increasing victory over the sexual chaos Jezebel seeks to bring to your inner life.*

---

* Space does not allow for full treatment of this subject. We have found other books such as *Surfing for God*, *Samson and the Pirate Monks*, and (for women) *No Stones* by Marnie Ferree to be helpful resources.

Preach the Gospel.
Die.
Be forgotten.

-Nicolas von Zinzendorf c. 1745

#ElijahMen

Focus: Jesus

'He must increase. I must decrease.' -Jn 3

What would you say is the heart of John's message? Is it *'sin is bad'*, *'repent or perish'*, *'share your clothes with those who don't have any'*, *'stop sleeping with your brother's wife'*, or *'God will judge the world'*? Those are bits and pieces of his message. But all those bullet points climax into something even greater. John is called to prepare a people for God's coming Messiah. As such, the heart of his message is *'Behold the Lamb of God that takes away the world's sin.'* (John 1)

Luke and Matthew also record a similar preaching climax to John's sermon in their gospels: *After me comes one whose sandals I am unworthy to untie.* As powerful in spirit as John is—and as big a splash as he makes—his final goal is not to draw people to himself. It is to lead people to be followers of Jesus. When John's disciples leave him to follow Jesus, he rejoices. He is a friend of the Bridegroom, he is not the Bridegroom himself.

Elijah did the same centuries earlier. His name and ministry were one: *Yahweh, He is God.* Elijah pointed people to the worship of Yahweh. John pointed people to follow the Christ. Yes, turning from idols, sexual immorality, and sin is a part of that. But it is just the first step. When we turn *from* something, we must turn *to* something. These prophets did not want people to turn from sin to moralism. They did not want people to turn from sin unto mere traditions. True repentance is turning *from* sin and *to* Jesus.

This is a point we must keep in mind: Elijah Men don't focus on Elijah. They focus on the one Elijah focused on. John's disciples didn't focus on John. They focused on the one he pointed them to.

This is not to say we shouldn't look to godly men as examples. That is, after all, what part of this book is about. We should look to others when they help us better follow Jesus. This is why it is written, *'Remember your leaders, who spoke the word of God to you. Consider the outcome of their way of life and imitate their faith'* (Heb. 13). Elijah qualifies as such a leader. This is why James encourages us in his epistle to see Elijah as an example in his praying.

158

John also qualifies. They both have spoken God's word over His people. We consider their way of life and imitate their faith in Jesus.

Do you aspire to be such a man to your generation? Do you want to be someone who speaks the word of God and lives a life of faith that others can imitate? Not so you can draw people into your own private following, but so that you can be part of Christ's visible Body here on Earth, pointing to the Head of the Body that is sitting in heaven. This is a good thing to aspire to. Being an Elijah Man does not mean wearing camel hair and starting your own little cult. It means living a life and sharing a message that points people away from idols and to this world's only Saviour.

Being a disciple, a son of the prophets, does not mean worshipping your own self-image as a holy man. This was the fault of the Pharisees. They were so focused on seeing themselves as disciples of Moses, they failed to worship from the heart the one whom Moses worshipped. Worship the God of Elijah. Do not be consumed with the Baptist. Be consumed with the One the Baptist was consumed with. Your personal vision should never be your own spiritual greatness. It is not to be of ourselves, preaching as a prophet. Our highest vision is of the Lamb, forgiving us as sinners.

Of Freedom & Foodolatry

'John's food was locusts and wild honey.' -Mt 3
'John's disciples fast.' -Mt 9

It may seem like a small point to us, but the Bible talks a lot about food. It takes time to not only mention that both Elijah and John ate food, but it also describes what they ate. Meat, wild honey, and bread were all on the menu. It also mentions that these men fasted.

Early in my days as a preacher, I thought that sex and gender-related issues were the most offensive things that one could talk about from the pulpit. After some time, I began to think that money was the most offensive. People seemed to be more upset when you told them what to do with their wallet than what to do with their genitals.

But now I think the subject that people get most defensive about is the food they eat. This makes a pastor's job a challenge as the Bible actually says a good deal about food. Sadly, some ministers cravenly fail to address this subject, fearing it will stir conflict. This is cowardice and doesn't actually serve the flock of God. It is also tragic as our generation has numerous problems with food ranging from anorexia and bulimia to the obesity epidemic that is destroying the health of millions in the UK, the USA, and many other Western countries. Some churches are good at addressing proper alcohol usage and the issue of drunkenness. But these same churches lack consistency in addressing food consumption. Most of what the Bible says about food can be placed in three broad categories.

Gratefulness

First of all, the Bible repeatedly instructs us to be grateful for our food. We are to receive it from God as a gift, not a right. We are to ask Him for 'our daily bread' and we are to be sincerely thankful when we get it. The Bible says that when Jesus took the fish and loaves, 'He looked up to heaven and gave thanks'. God could've made our physical absorption of nutrients a boring process. We could be created in such a way as to inject some dull, grey matter once a week to keep us going. Instead, we get to stop our work and have a celebration of God's goodness three times each day by enjoying the food he provides. Let's do more than say a token prayer of thanks before we eat. Come to the table to celebrate and be reminded of God's goodness and generosity.

Freedom

God's first word to Adam about food was one of freedom: *'You are free to eat from the trees of the garden'*. Only after establishing that freedom did he give the warning. The New Testament then goes on to teach that believers can now eat whatever food that God has created. Jesus had fulfilled the dietary cleanliness laws of Moses through his death. Paul writes to Timothy, *'For everything created by God is good, and nothing is to be rejected if it is received with gratitude'*. You want to eat whale? You can eat whale. Bacon? Yes. So long as you are thankful. Bear steak wrapped in bacon? A double amen. We may eat all God-created food with grateful hearts and we are not to judge those who eat differently than us.

Among other things, this means no divisive food philosophies. You want to eat paleo or vegetarian? Fine, but do not let it interfere with the table of Christian fellowship. When on mission, we are instructed by Jesus to *'eat what is set before you'*. This means that sometimes I eat something that I would not prefer or consider healthy for the sake of Christian unity or the sake of not giving offence. Relationships and witness are more important than the food we put in our body.

Our bodies are different and what one man can gratefully eat to maintain his health may be different to what I should gratefully eat to maintain my health. As Christians, we should all want to treat our God-given bodies with respect. But how we do that is a matter of individual conscience and liberty.

Wisdom

We enjoy our freedom, but we are instructed by the apostle, *'Do not use your freedom as an opportunity to indulge the flesh.'* That means that though we can eat whatever good, God created food is out there, we should not misuse that freedom. There are sins of gluttony and food idolatry. Proverbs notes, along with warnings of excessive alcohol, that *'It is not good to eat too much honey'*. If the wise men of the ancient world recognised that excessive amounts of natural sugars can be bad, how much more should we exercise caution in our day of refined sugar, glucose, and excessively processed food-like stuff?

Paul speaks of those whose *'god is their stomach'* and this foodolatry is as much an issue in our day as it was in his. We often eat too much. We eat man-made foods that have toxins, are addictive, and make our bodies susceptible to disease—all when we have the option of eating otherwise. We go to the refrigerator more than to the Bible when we are feeling low and need comfort. It's not by chance that 'food porn' is the banner under which attractive pictures of food on social media are tagged. Sadly, churches that take a firm stance on drunkenness often turn a blind eye to gluttony or reckless eating. Food is not sin. It is God's gift. So is alcohol. But the undisciplined use of either brings harm to our bodies and does not glorify God.

Christian discernment is also displayed by how we respond to trendy food advertising. Those who can exercise restraint in the face of photoshopped pics of sugar blondies may fall into the opposite trap of mindlessly paying extra for something merely because it has labels like 'diet', 'organic', or 'natural'. Since the fall in Eden, not everything 'natural' is necessarily good. Not everything processed is necessarily bad. It's wisdom to do our homework on foods that we regularly eat.

As Christians, we should eat to live, not live to eat. This is one of the reasons God's people throughout the Bible would have times of personal or corporate fasting—to make sure that their spiritual life was leading their fleshly life and not the other way around. Food is a great gift. But it is a cruel master. The wisdom of self-discipline will keep this good angel from becoming a taxing devil.

Food is a big theme throughout the Bible. Mankind first sinned through eating what it should not have and salvation is presented to us a meal of bread and wine. At the end of human history, a wedding feast awaits us. May we eat gratefully, freely, and wisely until that day.

Is Jesus Inclusive?

'He shall separate the wheat from the chaff.' -Lk 3

Inclusivity. It is the ethical word of our generation—the virtue by which every other virtue must be measured. Companies, political parties, and even celebrities vie to squeeze this word into their speeches. The search engine giant I use boasts that it is an 'inclusive place to work' and is trying to get the world reflect this value as well. Even churches get in on it. On my social media feed now I see things like 'Open Church Network' and 'The Inclusive Church' making waves. Everyone seemingly wants to be inclusive.

But amidst all this current enthusiasm of inclusivity, we are right to ask: Did John seek to be inclusive? Did Elijah? And, more importantly, is the God that these men point to *inclusive*?

It depends on how we use the term. 'Inclusive' is a fuzzy term. The Serpent loves fuzzy words and ideas. They let him say one thing yet mean another. Jezebel delights in fuzzy words because it allows her to say the same thing yet mean it in two different ways creating room for double standards that most people at first assume are completely legitimate. But Elijah Men love dictionaries. Prophets tend to be straight shooters who mean what they say. And if a dictionary records more than one meaning for a word, they will not be shy to state which sense they are utilising.

If by inclusive we mean 'hospitable', then yes, Jesus was inclusive. We are to welcome people into our churches and homes who are outsiders. We are to give people who are different from us hot cups of coffee, a listening ear, and comfortable chairs to sit in. We should be kind to them whether they are rich or poor. We are to preach, give announcements, and interact using language that is intelligible to outsiders so that our witness can be clear to all. There is a tendency for churches to become inward looking over time. They can become clubs that only care for its own membership rather than a movement that exists to rescue outsiders. We must seek to rescue brown, white and black, male and female, young and old, etc. If by *inclusive* we mean hospitable, yes, and a thousand times so.

But there is another sense in which the gospel is very exclusive. Elijah's name means '*Yahweh is God*'—as opposed to any others. He sought to bring back Israel to the worship of Yahweh alone and not to include Baal alongside Him. When John introduces Jesus, it is as one who separates '*the wheat from the chaff*'. Jesus himself often spoke of separating people, not bringing them together. He spoke of separating the nations into sheep and goats. He spoke of ten virgins: five who he would leave out as foolish and five whom he would receive as wise. He spoke of branches that did not bear fruit that he would cast into the fire as opposed to branches that did bear fruit—ones that he would keep and prune.

There are servants he rewards and servants he casts into outer darkness. He said we must enter through the narrow gate, because many people walk on the broad road to destruction. It is hard to imagine how Jesus could have been any clearer: some will be welcomed into his Kingdom, and some will not be. We read of him excluding as much as he is including. Our greatest priority must be to be among those who are included—and to call others to that path.

This is why we need to be clear in our thinking when we speak about preaching '*an inclusive gospel*' as some do. Jezebel is sly and she knows how to tweak a good word to a perverse end. An inclusive gospel that is pleasing to God is one that says anyone is welcome to repent and find forgiveness in Jesus and share communion at our table. Race, economic status, gender—none of this keeps you out of God's Kingdom. Only sin keeps us out and it is sin that Jesus has come to remove. Everything can be cleansed and washed away. Are you a practising paedophile? A Nazi? A gossip? A Marxist? A violent person? If you renounce the practice of your evil deeds and cast yourself on the mercy of the Cross you can be pure as snow—come and eat with us. Come liars, come thieves, come adulterers, come pornographers, come corrupt bank CEOs! Come all you practising homosexuals, you fornicators, you slanderers, you whores, you judgmental moralists, you abusers, and all you dearly loved bastards. Come to the table of the Lord. Leave your sin and be transformed.

Christ's inclusivity takes anyone from any background and transforms them into a child of God. He can take any unholy man and make him holy. This gospel affirms that God loves you in spite of who you are. Our sins have damned us. Every one of us is excluded from the start. But Jesus has paid the cost of his blood to lift us out of our bed of consequences. He was excluded in death so that we could be included in Life. He will exclude the proud who believe that they aren't sinners in need of a Saviour. But he will include all those who come to him in humility and repentance—those he will never reject.

Jezebel's inclusivity leaves you without the repentance and transformation. It tells you that God doesn't mind your sin. It affirms you as a sinner and leaves you the way you are. There is no offence in the Jezebel message—no blow to the Adamic ego. It does not call for the death of the inner rebellion that we all instinctively have towards God and his Law. We must expose as fake any gospel that includes spiritually dead people without also transforming them. We are in the business of telling goats how they can be born again as sheep—not simply telling goats they are fine just as they are.

Job Vacancy: Prophet

'Who did you go into the wilderness expecting to see? A reed blown about by the wind or a man in soft clothing?' -Mt 11

John was an Elijah Man in many ways. Both men ate meat. Elijah's meat flew to him courtesy of Raven Airways. John's meat flew to him with its own wings: he ate locust (which doesn't sound great but it's supposed to be uber-high in protein—plus John dipped his in wild honey which could be used as a type of BBQ sauce; all very paleo).

Like Elijah, John also lived in the desert. Both men were preachers. Neither man was 'balanced'. Both men had hungry young men following them. Both had a powerful woman trying to kill them. Both were followed by someone with considerably better people skills. Like Elijah, John had a life of fervent prayer and fasting—not just for his own contemplative purposes, but to do battle for the destiny of a nation. Half an hour before Elijah spoke before Ahab, no one anticipated his prophetic cry. Before John the Baptist opened his mouth, there was no one in Jerusalem who knew he was there. (Half an hour after he proclaimed that word, there was no one who didn't.)

John stepped into a spiritually barren desert. Herod and his lascivious lady reigned with Roman power and paraded their sexual immorality. The Romans proudly portrayed their paganism up and down the land allotted to God's people. The Pharisees retreated into a cavern of fundamentalist orthodoxy but failed to shed a tear for those on the outside. The progressive Sadducees tried to make room for both their inherited allegiance to Yahweh and the powers and cultural ideas of the new Roman learning.

It seemed like any type of God honouring ministry would be impossible in such a place. The blind were horsewhipping the blind. It was black midnight on the spiritual landscape. And then the heavens opened and the mega-word spoken by this strange desert child was downloaded onto the nation with a power and speed that our current internet bandwidths can only envy.

The English-speaking church has a vacancy that needs filling. God's Church in the UK has an opening and it is urgent that there are men who step into it. The role of prophet is wide open. With all our technology, money, and conferences, it is still (with occasional exception) getting darker. Baal and Asherah are worshipped in the Temple of God under deceptively worded but colourful banners. The fake teachings are old but they're repackaged for a new generation. They are pedlars pimping out fake love, fake justice, and affirming people in their bondage instead of setting them free from it.

We have meetings aplenty but none of them seem to rock society at large or introduce the Fear of the Lord (a concept the Church has seemingly forgotten) into the world around us. Where is the spoken word which will cause people to say of us, as they did the early church, *these men have turned the world upside down*? With all our activity, we need one who can wield a word which will shake a nation. But who is fit to speak such a word? Britain needs broken, godly men to break the hearts of wicked men. He who would reap with joy must first sow in tears. The lifespan of men in the Bible who carried the word of repentance was noticeably short. Those who would call sin, 'sin' better not value too much this present life with all its toys, accolades and comforts. Men who seek to fill this role will be familiar with much private prayer and fasting. It is these men who fast that feast at the tables of wholeheartedness.

I am thankful for our Bible colleges. God does not put a high value on ignorance. But though the Church has never had more men (and women) with such high levels of education than it does now, we are still losing ground with every decade. We have many people with great intellectual stature, but few of equal spiritual stature.

To qualify for the role of prophet, there is no requirement of formal education. There is, however, the requirement that you '*have been with Jesus*' (Acts 4). Your life must be wholly his. All your treasure must be stored up with him. You cannot be one who is shaken by the tremors of time but you must tremble before Eternity's throne. There is no pay. It will cost you everything. Your heart will break and you may not live to retirement. Great rewards will be in heaven. Please send your job application along with your sweat, blood, and tears to: The Altar of God. If selected, the world will know.

It's true that many are praying for a worldwide revival. But it would be timelier, and more scriptural, for prayer to be made to the Lord of the harvest, that He would raise up and thrust forth labourers who would fearlessly and faithfully preach those truths which are calculated to bring about a revival.

- A. W. Pink

#ElijahMen

Three Prophets Walk into a Bar

'The boy will be a Nazarite from birth—and he will start to save Israel.' -Jg 13

Three prophets walk into a bar. All three eat meat, but only one can have a drink. His name is Elijah. The two teetotallers are John the Baptist and Samson. This last chap may seem rather out of place to bring into our discussion on Elijah. But if we will take a closer look, we will see some similarities and contrasts.

Only two men in Scripture were called to be Nazarites in regards to alcohol—John and Samson. Elijah was a disciplined man—but he could have a whisky if and when he wanted. (I like to think Elijah takes a spicy Canadian rye instead of its more mellow Scotch cousin, but I'm aware that, doctrinally, this may be a secondary issue.)

All three of these men had a *femme fatale* in their lives. Jezebel attempted to kill Elijah. Herodias did kill John. And Delilah led Samson to his ruin. The course of their lives was partially determined by how they related to these bewitching beauties. All three men also had a healthy relationship with at least one woman. Samson and John both had godly mothers that are part of their stories. Likewise, Elijah had the Phoenician widow as a friend. They received encouragement from these women of faith. Elijah and Samson both see great miracles—the first through a variety of spectacular signs and the second through his Hulk-like strength. John was a bit different. He never performed a miracle in that sense. Unlike Elijah, he never did raise a dead boy. But that doesn't mean he's without the Ghost. Hardly. John raised a dead nation.

Also, all three stepped onto the scene when things were dark. They were men who were sent to deliver the people of God from the dire consequences of their own apostasy. All three were strong and rugged men. Samson tore a lion in half with his bare hands—it's hard to top that as dinner table stories go.

But Samson is different from the other two because—though mighty and masculine—there is tragedy written all over his life. And this needs to stand as a warning to us men who desire to be used by God in dark times. Samson began well. We could applaud his debut battle with the Philistines. The Kingdom is filled with many great starters. But it's how we finish that's of greater importance.

I remember one great champion of the faith. He preached crusades, called thousands to repentance, and challenged Jezebel in his generation. He thundered against the works of darkness.

I was just a child when his fall into sin became public. But I still have a dim memory of it making the news. He was caught with a prostitute. Years later the full story came out. He had been waging a war on pornography. While deciding which magazines were truly pornographic or not he became addicted to the very material he was fighting. That led to a downward spiral of addiction that led him to a hotel room with a commercial sex worker. The darkness he warred against found a back door into his own life—and it devoured him.

Samson was called to be a judge among God's people, to lead them in holiness and protect them from evil forces without. But Samson's saga is a shipwreck. He fought against the darkness in the world, but he couldn't get victory over the darkness inside of him. He was conquering in public while losing in private. Elijah fought against the influences of Jezebel. John fought against the influences of Herodias, but Samson let himself be seduced by Delilah. Had he graciously reached out in a godly way to a pagan woman as Elijah did, that would have been praiseworthy. But instead of him leading a lost woman into godliness, he let her lead him into sin.

It is possible to be attacking Jezebellic strongholds with our words on the exterior while also being eaten up by her vexing viruses on the interior. This is not to say that we must arrive at sinless perfection before God can use us. But God's men must live lives of continual repentance. Have a trusted friend to confess openly to. Sin may come, but we must quickly war against it when it does. Elijah's earthly life ended with him being carried to heaven in a chariot of fire while Samson met his end being buried in the rubble of a pagan temple. He was called to do the works of an Elijah. But he never outgrew the heart of an Ahab. The difference was how they dealt with private sin.

Jesus: the Greater Elijah

'Who do men say that I am?' -Jesus
'Some say Elijah.' – Peter

How is Elijah connected with Jesus? Should we see ourselves as disciples of Elijah, or only as disciples of Jesus?

Do you remember the account where Jesus contrasts his ministry with that of John the Baptist? In both Matthew 11 and Luke 7 Jesus speaks to the crowds about how some of their leaders dismissed John as a demon because he seemingly fasted too much and lived in the desert. By contrast, Jesus spends much of his time eating, drinking, and telling his parables at dinner parties and spending time in town.

And to be sure, there is a clear difference. One is the King, and the other is the prophet that points to the King. One is from heaven, one is from earth. One forgives and saves, the other points to that one. Jesus taught that fasting was inappropriate for his disciples to do because he was already with them in all his fulness—it was a time of celebration. This is the difference between the two in terms of creation and Creator. And many commentators have also noted how Jesus' style is more reminiscent of Elisha, Elijah's successor, while Elijah's style of ministry seems to prefigure John.

But if we only focus on the differences, we lose something of our understanding of both Elijah and Jesus. We may even start to think of Elijah as an angry kid who didn't play well with others, hung out with birds, and ate meat all day while Jesus is the chilled guy who hangs out at parties, sips his lattes, never raises his voice, is vegetarian, and is all together down with the cool kids. If this is our stereotype—if we fail to see Jesus as the greater Elijah—then we do not really get Jesus.

And Jesus isn't a vegetarian.

When Jesus asked Peter who the crowds thought that he was, Peter responded that some thought he was the return of Elijah. If Jesus was just the guy in shades who swapped the latest music with his friends and *only* talked about how God was a really nice guy, how then did he leave people with that Elijah-like impression? How exactly did some people mistake Jesus for Elijah 2.0?

A close look a Jesus' ministry shows it was similar to Elijah's in many respects. As followers of Jesus we need to grasp the overlap. There are certainly two similarities that would've stood out to the crowds. First of all, both Elijah's and Jesus' ministries were marked by a strong message of repentance. Both insisted that men must turn from darkness to the light of God. At times, this message was confrontational in its quest to persuade.

Secondly, there was the ministry of power. Both Elijah and Jesus performed mighty, public miracles. I realise that our readers will have a variety of views on things like 'the gifts of the Spirit'. It is beyond the scope of this book to do a study on big words like 'continuationism' and 'cessastionism'. We would inevitably get tossed around and begin to get off track. I have known godly men and evangelists who professed both views of the spiritual gifts and who were used strongly by God to see souls saved. But though these men professed different beliefs in the gifts, both groups were men of faith that depended on the workings of God and not those of the flesh.

However God's power works, we are in desperate need of it. We need the Ghost. Paul said that his gospel didn't just come with *'persuasive words, but in the demonstration of the Spirit's power.'* Preacher, do your sermons come in word only? Or, is there the clear mark of the Ghost in your ministry? Our days are not less wicked than Elijah's or Paul's. We need men of faith that can pray and see answers. John the Baptist had no visible miracles, but his preaching carried the power of another world and it awoke Israel. Is there something supernatural about our lives? Or, could it all be imitated in the flesh?

A bold call to repentance and a Spirit-empowered ministry were the two big similarities of Jesus' and Elijah's public ministry that could have led to some confusion. They are also two things sorely lacking in the British church at the moment (and probably the church in many other lands as well). But a closer look at their private lives reveals there was more than just these things. Both men had deep lives of private prayer. Both men were kind and gentle with the weak, foreigners, and those with sincere questions. Both men firmly, yet respectfully, spoke the truth to rulers who were swayed by external forces: Elijah to Ahab and Jesus to Pilate.

There was no competition between John and Jesus' ministry. In time, John's disciples began to focus more and more on Jesus. And this is what John wanted. There is much we can learn from Elijah's life about how we can better follow Christ—both his grace empowered successes as well as his grace forgiven faults. Letting the example of his life disciple us correctly, will help us be better disciples of Christ.

Elijah and the Spoken Word

'Listen to him.'-Lk 9

Jesus takes his three top disciples up Mt. Hermon. Perhaps Peter, James, and John thought they were going to get some rest with Jesus. Their rabbi had been speaking to the crowds about crucifixion—a subject they didn't understand much. Perhaps while on the mountain Jesus would explain himself a bit better. They get to the top and Jesus begins to pray. The others begin to snooze. Nothing new to see here.

But then something changes. Jesus changes. He gets all LED. No, this is not a dream. Moses and Elijah show up and start talking with Jesus—not from the past, but from paradise. This is probably when the disciples realised it was not going to be a typical lazy afternoon. *Here is Elijah! Here is Moses!* The great men of faith they had grown up hearing about were right in front of them. Glory was shining. This is not the first time Jesus met with Elijah on a mountain. Remember Horeb? It's not the first time he met Moses on a mountain either. Remember Sinai? Both men now taste a greater glory on this mountain as they speak with Jesus about his approaching death.

A cloud comes down on the mountain. The Father, is there. The disciples may wonder if they will hear the Ten Commandments given again to Moses or if Elijah will again hear the whispered words more wonderful than the wild winds which whipped Horeb. They do hear a voice. But it is neither of those things from the past. Instead it says, *'This is my Son, my chosen. Listen to him.'*

Then Jesus is alone. The Prophet and the Law Giver are back up in glory. But Jesus must now descend. Though he could call a legion of celestial chariots to take him back up to the Father's side, he forgoes that. He is preparing, not for a fiery taxi like Elijah took, but for a fiery baptism. This is what Jesus spoke to the crowds about. It is not enough for the disciples to see the glory of God on the mountain. They need to understand what it all means. This requires ears, not eyes. They need to understand the Cross. This is what they needed to listen to. It is also what this generation needs to hear.

174

Words are essential to our witness. As great as serving projects are, as great as signs and wonders are, as great as the carefully laid ambience of a worship service may be, none of them by themselves explain who Jesus is and why he had to die. If a person is to be saved, they must hear a message. As Paul will later write in Romans, '*How can they believe on him of whom they have not heard? And how can they hear without a preacher?*' Jesus did not leave behind a portrait of himself. He left behind his words. In our virtual reality generation, it is Spirit-empowered words that confront people with Ultimate Truth.

If we are to see revival and reformation in our lives and churches, we must regain cross-centred preaching. Nothing is wrong with having nice art in your church to look at. Nothing is wrong with having quality coffee to smell and taste. But God has ordained words to be the vehicle for making a man or woman new. Jesus is 'the Word' become flesh. People will behold the Cross—but it will take words to explain it.

So many talks I hear in churches across our nation are without a cross. The main point of sermons in many of our British congregations are merely moral messages that would get an 'amen' in a mosque or in a synagogue. We often give good advice instead of good news. We tell people what to do. *Don't drink too much. Recycle and care for the planet. Don't have sex with that person. Stop taking drugs. Don't vote Tory. Don't vote Labour. Etc.* We talk about spirituality, community ethics, and morality. We speak little of the Cross.

It is not wrong to give good advice. We can give parenting classes and financial management courses. But none of it will bring revival. None of it will draw a life closer to God. Not even saying '*Jesus died on a cross*' is sufficient. The Cross must be explained. It is written that the gospel is *the power of God for salvation.* Perhaps if we are not seeing God's power in salvation, it is because we are not faithfully and prayerfully proclaiming the gospel.

Elijah heard a helpful whisper on Horeb. He now hears an even better word on Hermon. He hears that Christ is about to pay for his sins, the sins of Elisha, the sins of the widow, and sins of the whole world. This is the word we must hear—and the word we must share.

Elijah was a man.

-James 5

#ElijahMen

♂♀ Intro

Studying Elijah, Ahab, and Jezebel in our current cultural milieu inevitably brings up gender related questions. In the next three readings, we're going to ask some of them. Now it would be terribly unfair if this author were to address a hugely controversial issue like this and not be willing to reveal his own personal and theological cards. We are all biased. Only liars and fools claim not to be. So for integrity sake, I wish to at least put my bias on the table for all to see. If you're new to this discussion, welcome. I use some big, technical terms. Feel free to pause a moment to google them if they are unfamiliar.
We all have our stories, here is mine.

I was raised in an Egalitarian denomination that ordained women. The General Superintendent of that denomination is currently a woman. In my teen years, I switched denominations. This one was also Egalitarian, but admittedly more so in theory than in common practice. I never had 'Mother God' ideology shoved down my throat. After high-school, I spent one year assisting a female pastor and saw many people make professions for Christ and grow in discipleship. I have good memories from that time.

In the first few years of marriage, my wife and I were missionaries in France. During this time, gender issues came up as a point of controversy. The Norwegian missionaries we worked with were generally more Egalitarian while the French believers were generally more Complementarian or even Patriarchal. At first, we entered the discussions to argue for Egalitarianism. But as we began to engage with thoughtful leaders who were not Feminists, we realised that we had some simple strawman stereotypes. Though there may have been the occasional chauvinist, the vast majority of French Complementarian church leaders that we met were hungry for God's daughters to arise with their gifts and pounce on the works of the darkness. They simply believed the role of an elder was a governmental one reserved for qualified men. I now look back with shame at some of the misrepresentations that I used to portray classical Christian beliefs on this point of gender roles.

Clearly there was some thinking here that was more nuanced than what I had been previously acknowledged. Over time, and with lots of conversations, we became convinced that the Egalitarian perspective was not based on the best exposition of Scripture. We reluctantly adopted a moderate Complementarian view.

But we are no longer reluctant. Today we see this perspective as beautiful and we enjoy being faithful to it the best we can (though I am often still pretty bad at it). We should note here that there is a huge difference between seeing God affirm gender uniqueness in Scripture and embracing wider culture's notions of gender roles. As stated in a previous reading, some things that go under the banner of 'Patriarchy' should indeed be smashed. I do not naturally gravitate towards some of the masculine stereotypes that culture holds to. I do not generally enjoy playing or watching sports. I enjoy reading good poetry far more. I am naturally more of a shopper than my wife is. The first couple years of our marriage I dominated the kitchen as I like to cook and am quite comfortable there. I still am.

We also recognise that God works through many Egalitarian ministries. Biblical church order should be something we pursue, but our church structure doesn't have to be perfect in order for God's grace to work in saving ways through us. Though the church I pastor embraces male eldership as a rule, we also have active female deacons who are essential to the fruitfulness of our work. We work to encourage all believers, male and female, to use their gifts in the spheres where God has them. I have many books on my kindle and shelves written by women and I learn much from them.

But these readings are not about explaining Complementarianism. Let's put our big boy trousers on and ask some hard questions. Well start with MRA or 'Menism'.

♂♀ Part One

'I do not permit a woman to teach and have authority over a man.' -1Tim 2
'Wives, submit to your husbands. Husbands, love your wives.' -Col 3

<u>Trigger Warning</u>: *We're going to talk about gender now because, you know, this book hasn't been controversial enough. This is the first of three parts that take a look at both Menism and Feminism. If you get triggered easily, please take your meds before reading.*

Red Pill is a documentary that was released in 2016 by filmmaker Cassie Jaye who has produced other award-winning documentaries. But this one is different. Through the film, Miss Jaye undergoes a transformation. She begins the film as a Feminist who is out to expose the insidious Men's Rights Activists (MRA). But in the process, she becomes convinced that the movement is not composed of misogynistic thugs as she had previously been led to believe. Miss Jaye concludes that it is her own Feminist ideology that is errant, abandons it, and embraces *Menism*. Needless to say, the film stirred up lots of controversy. Various anti-free speech groups and Feminist allies tried to have the film boycotted and were successful in causing some cancellations. But the film started leaking out and meaningful discussions and debate around the issues of began taking place.

Though I greatly appreciate *Red Pill* for exposing the monstrous hypocrisy of modern, Western Feminism in such a brilliant fashion, we need to draw a distinction between the MRA movement and what Scripture calls us to in regards to gender. Jezebel seeks to mislead us into both fake spirituality and fake gender understanding and we need to have our thinking shaped by Scripture and not by Feminism or MRA.

Elijah Men are not MRA

Like Miss Jaye, we might assume that Elijah would be a Menist. *This rough and rugged man is certainly MRA material, right?* Perhaps not. When we look close we can see that MRA is an Egalitarian movement by seeking to bring equality between men and women through laws, policies, and role equalisation. They point out those areas of society where men may have been seen to be treated unfairly or oppressed. They focus on facts such as,

- Many child custody laws favour the mother over the father

- 98% of all combat deaths are male
- 93% of all workplace deaths are male
- Men are three times as likely to be homeless
- Men are four times as likely to commit suicide
- Women are 35% more likely to go to University
- Women retire 2 years earlier than men, even though they live 2.7 years longer—giving them almost 5 years more retirement years.

Menism believes that third-wave Feminism went too far and now their actions often discriminate against men. They seek the type of equality that many Feminist organisations claim to. They point out how most Feminist organisations turn a blind eye whenever a law or social trend favours women over men. MRA seeks to equalise the stats.

Christians may applaud MRA for ideologically seeking to balance Feminism, but we are fundamentally different from Menism. We do not seek equality through stats. We are not seeking role interchangeability. We do not object to men laying down their lives on the battlefield for their wives back home nor do we object to the fact that more women than men chose to stay home to raise children.

As Christians, we celebrate gender uniqueness. Gender is the wonderful distinction God put into humanity in Genesis one. God made men and women different. Each gender has its own unique set of blessings and challenges and jealously trying to trade one set of challenges or blessings for the other is called covetousness—a sin in case you're rusty.

Satan wants us to dismiss the beauty of God's gender binary. This is because the mystery of gender uniqueness proclaims God's redemptive purpose for humanity. In Ephesians 5 we read how man and woman in marriage is to reflect Christ and his church. Unlike MRA, we do not seek to erase differences or to obtain equality through even numbers of males and females represented in every area of society. We believe that men and women are equal—and always have been—because our value comes from God. He has made us both his image bearers. Until MRA and Feminists discover where our value comes from, neither side will ever be happy with new legislation passed and they will continue to keep their supporters trapped in a perpetual sense of victimhood to keep their machinery running.

♂♀ Part Two

'I do not permit a woman to teach and have authority over a man.' -1Tim 2
'Wives, submit to your husbands. Husbands, love your wives.' -Col 3

On the 20th March, 2014 Labour MP Ben Bradshaw of Exeter stood in Parliament and gave a speech commemorating the 20th anniversary of the ordination of women in the Church of England. Reflecting on the issue as a Catholic, he proclaimed,

> *I confidently expect the Roman Catholic Church to embrace the ministry of women, in exactly the same way as the Church of England has done. It is a theological inevitability. It may not happen in my lifetime, but the fact that we have done it, blazed a trail and shown how positive, successful, valuable, wonderful and holy it is will help progressive Catholics on the same road.*[*]

Two elements of this speech are noteworthy. The first is the confident assertion that this change was a '*successful*' one. The second is the view that all of Christianity will fall into line with this '*theological inevitability*'.

What is the fruit of Theological Feminism?

A couple generations ago, some denominations embraced theological Feminism (TF). We acknowledge this is a huge umbrella term. On the shallow end, TF includes married pastoral couples where the husband and wife are ordained together. These churches are mildly Egalitarian and are typical of some Pentecostal denominations (think Brian and Bobby Houston of Hillsong) that donot hold to gender roles in the church but often do in the home. The husband still does most of the preaching and is seen as the 'lead' pastor, but the wife also carries the title pastor even if hers is a more supportive role. This Egalitarianism is the shallow end of the TF pool.

---

[*]http://www.benbradshaw.co.uk/speech_on_20th_anniversary_of_the_ordination_of_women

There are many expressions of Pentecostalism so the degree of Feminist influence varies, but the general trend of the last 20 years has been towards Egalitarianism. One of the biggest shifts is that of the Vineyard movement which was started by John Wimber in 1984. Wimber drew a clear line between 'ministering' (which all Christians are called to) and executive 'governing' which only elders (qualified men) do. In 1994 he wrote,

I believe God has established a gender based eldership of the church…
I endorse the traditional (and what I consider Scriptural) view of a unique leadership role for men in marriage, family, and in the church…Consequently, I do not favor ordaining women as elders in the local church.[*]

Current Vineyard leadership has slowly departed from Wimber's instruction and now ordains women as both elders and lead pastors. Other denominations practice this more widely. These include churches where the lead pastor is female and is unmarried, married to an unbeliever, or has a Christian husband under her authority in the congregation.

But we can't stop here. The TF pool gets deeper still. There are churches where leaders openly refer to God as 'Mother' in their prayers, worship, and liturgy. One group, 'Priests for Equality' have printed *The Inclusive Bible* that refers to God as both *He* and *She* and changes some of the masculine references to God. These theological Feminists hate gender and try to minimise it whenever they can. These are the ones who want you to trade in your 'he' and 'she' pronouns for a neutered 'ze'. They loathe the fact that God chose to become incarnate as a male and seek to present him in more androgynous ways. One wonders if they would not castrate Christ if they could. There are many at the shallow end of the TF pool, mild Egalitarians, that would disassociate themselves with what goes on at the deeper end.

TF History

How has all this happened?[†] Canadian professor Mary Kassian points out that the TF movement emerged alongside secular Feminism[‡] which has as

---

[*] *Liberating Women for Ministry and Leadership*, Vineyard Reflections, March/April 1994

[†] Mary Kassian has well documented the effects of Feminism on the 20th Century church.

[‡] We happy acknowledge that Feminism has changed over the decades. Most divide Feminism into three phases: 1st, 2nd, and 3rd Wave Feminism. There are many Christians who would be rightful sympathetic to the goals of equality by the early Feminists but reject the blurring of gender distinctions by 3rd Wave Feminists.

one of its aims the blurring of gender distinctions. In the 70s, it was packaged as a version of Liberation Theology and still is in some circles.

This new ideology promised that by treating men and women as interchangeable in all ministry (and later family) roles, the church would become more fruitful. It was the Bishop of Bristol, Barry Rogerson, who led the first ordination service for women in the Church of England (CoE) where he cited Jesus *By their fruits you will know them.* The meaning was clear: the CoE would now be more fruitful with women vicars. His speech was not unusual. Many had been saying that adopting Feminist practices we would usher in a new day of fruitfulness. It was promised that, by becoming gender-blind, we would inaugurate a new day of effectively engaging wider society with the gospel. Numbers had been slipping and TF would now be the saving life force that would turn the tide.

What did it look like practically? Constance Coltman was the first woman to be ordained in a major Protestant church here in the UK 100 years ago in 1917. Her church was part of the Congregational movement that had become forerunners in theological liberalism. Today this denomination is known as the URC (United Reformed Church). Methodism—which had a long tradition of permitting women to preach—started actually ordaining women as presbyters in 1974. And it was in 1994 that the Church of England started ordaining women—17 years later than their American Episcopal cousins. The CoE has worked at making up for lost time and now ordains close to the same number of men and women each year. The Methodists were the first to use a liturgy that addressed God as Mum. The CoE followed their example a few years later.

What does the data say?

How did this decision impact these large British denominations? Did the new dawn of gender understanding deliver the growth and robust health as promised? If we are to take Bishop Rogerson's invitation to judge this new practice by its fruit, what conclusion should we come to 20+ years later? Did the Mummy God that some started praying to send revival?

Affirming data is simply not there. Statistics show that theological Feminism lied. It failed to keep its promises. Numbers continued to go down. Anglican attendance is now 65% of what it was in 1994. Sunday attendance in Methodist churches is only 25% of what it was in 1974 and the URC figures are not much different (the URC statistics we've seen count membership, not attendance, but the same rapid loss is reflected). On top of that, URC and Methodism have the oldest average age of attendees of any denomination with the Anglicans not far behind. What happened to Feminism helping the church reach the cutting edge of the new secular culture? Statistics seem to go in the opposite direction of the common rhetoric which asserts, '*You need to give up your old, conservative views of gender and sexuality or else all your young people will leave your churches and never come back.*' It's commonly heard, but we struggle to find data that backs up such assertions.

It is hard to discern just how embracing TF has helped us be an Elijahian witness in a dark and perverse world. Yes, there are some good men and women in those denominations doing good work. We could find exceptions to these trends. But as a whole, TF has not reversed the downward spiral and, though such a hypothesis is beyond the scope of this reading to analyse, some argue that it may have accelerated the decline.

Not only has attendance in all of these denominations plummeted and aged, but on average now, only 38% of those in attendance are male—and few theological Feminists that we encounter seem to have a problem with this. In fact, some still claim their denominations have not gone far enough in '*smashing the patriarchy*'.

True of all Religions?
It should be noted that this trend is not true of all religious groups in the UK. It should not be assumed that all religions or Christian denominations have seen equal decline under the general influence of secularisation. The Pentecostal grouping (which includes both mild Egalitarian and Complementarian), has actually grown nearly 25% during this same time. Other non-Feminist church movements have also seen growth.

All this leads us to ask if MP Bradshaw's statement regarding the huge '*success*' of the CoE's ordination of women and the '*theological inevitability*' of all branches of Christianity embracing such a position is a well-founded statement. One wonders what type of statistical analysis he used to reach such a conclusion.

Now some may say: *But embracing TF or rejecting it should not be based on 'numbers'. It should be based on the clear teaching of Scripture!* I'm glad you brought that up. The two are separate but not mutually exclusive issues. God's work done God's way produces godly fruit. It is beyond what we can

184

do in a short reading to give a full exposition of all the relevant passages of Scripture. There are much better books by smarter authors who have already done so. Simply stated, 95% of Christians through 95% of church history (at least!) have not understood the Bible to teach TF. No, there has not always been total agreement through the Centuries on all gender issues. The Angles and the Saxons gave more authority to female church leaders in the 5th-10th Centuries than what we see after the Norman invasion of 1066. But even under the more flexible Angles and the Saxons, there was still a role of oversight (Bishops) reserved for qualified men who functioned as spiritual fathers in the church. Even then, gender roles were never taught to be fully interchangeable in the church or the home. Until now.

We ask if the presence of modern TF in the church has made a noticeable difference in helping the church to be a holy, growing force in the world that aggressively kicks down the gates of hell through the bold preaching of the gospel. Based on any unbiased research, is this really the case? If anyone knows of a large denomination that has seen accelerated growth after embracing TF, please email us the details and we will make fair note of this example.

Until now, we simply haven't come across any.

♂♀ Part Three

'I do not permit a woman to teach and have authority over a man.' -1Tim 2
'Wives, submit to your husbands. Husbands, love your wives.' -Col 3

Feminism and LGBTism in the Church

If you didn't burn the book after the last reading, well done. Perhaps you are a Feminist who has dared to go outside your echo chamber by reading this—that's exceptional. At least you are open-minded enough to explore relevant questions and objections to your beliefs. Well done.

Here is another question: *Why are the denominations that embraced Feminism a generation or two ago now being invaded by LGBT activism but not the ones that didn't?* Earlier this year, it was the URC who marked their 100th anniversary of ordaining women with a call to all churches to start 'marrying' gay couples. There is great pressure within Methodism and CoE to do the same.

If you identify as an 'Egalitarian' who also embraces the historic, Christian understanding of marriage between one man and one woman, ask yourself why Complementarian or Patriarchal denominations have so little internal trouble in resisting the pressure to capitulate to LGBT activism while the TF ones (CoE, URC, Methodism, etc) are struggling to stay faithful on this point? Why do you think that is? Not only have FIEC, New Frontiers, Roman Catholicism, AMiE, Eastern Orthodoxy, large segments of Pentecostalism, and other non-Feminist denominations generally avoided the huge drop in attendance over the last few decades (some have actually grown) but they are not being overrun by Rainbow Jihadis either.

Could it be that the same questionable hermeneutics used to dismiss passages that support gender roles in the church and the home are now being used on marital relationships? Some think so—and it is worth publicly discussing the issue. Let's have some fair and open talk on the connection.

Perhaps TF's most devastating legacy is that, just like John prepared the way for Christ, so TF prepared the way for something bigger than itself. TF has prepared the path for LGBTism. Denominations that were infected with this ideological virus are now faced with the next logical step. *'Since a woman can be a bishop or a pastor, why not a husband and father too? Why can't a man be*

We need at this time rulers in the Church who can add to the force, flame, and fragrance of Elijah's praying by their own prayers.

-EM Bounds

#ElijahMen

a wife or mother?' The questions are fair. If we base titles only on perceived ability—with gender never being a factor—why bar a woman from being a husband or dad if she claims she can do it? Isn't that *'gender discrimination'*?

Yes, it is. And the churches in the UK, USA and the West are in great need of godly gender discrimination once again. This does not mean we value one gender above the other. To discriminate (from the Latin *discriminat* : to distinguish between) means we are able to discern the unique beauty and calling God has put in us respectively as men and women. When we can discriminate between the genders in a godly way we can see why the Biblical view of marriage makes sense. It is a sacrament pointing to Christ and his church. Marriage was created—not just to give us romantic goose bumps—but to give humanity a picture of the gospel.

Denominations that did not give into TF a generation ago are not being divided by the current winds and waves of queer theology. The ones that did are now wrecked by its legitimate ideological heir.

Come back Peter, Come back Paul

LGBT theological activism is not an overwhelming, internal issue for most professing Christian denominations. It is not an internal issue because most denominations are not intoxicated by the wine of Feminism. Out of the three branches of Christianity—Catholic, Protestant, and Orthodox—it is only Protestantism that has opened itself to Feminism to this degree. Catholicism and Eastern Orthodoxy (for whatever other theological problems they may have) have at least resisted this modern impulse. It is only a segment of Protestantism that has experimented with TF—though this segment is disproportionately larger here in the UK than it is in many other nations.

In our quest for revival and reformation, at some point we will need to go back to what Paul and Peter said about gender roles and sexuality in their epistles. We need to see what commands they gave to men and what commands they gave to women—and we need to take them seriously. Instructions were given to *husbands* or to *wives*. They were rarely given to *spouses* generically. The Bible could have given us instructions for *clergy spouses*. But it doesn't. It gives us instructions for *elders* and *elders' wives*.

To love the widow and her son well, Elijah did not have to become a Feminist. He needed to be a friend.

✎

trying to get inside to wield influence and usurp authority within. Though the taste of Christian blood is sweet to hell, the taste of a Christian's decaying holiness is far sweeter. As nice as it is to persecute God's men from the outside, demons relish seeing them fall into sexual and spiritual compromise far more.

Jezebel's voice is ringing in the 21st Century Western church. It can be heard campaigning in synods and echoing on your social media page. But what about Elijah's voice? When was the last time your church gave clear teaching on Biblical sex? Most young Christians see little reason to object to sex before marriage. We excuse fornication by saying, '*They really love each other. They'll probably get married anyway.*' There is also little backbone to confront LGBT ideology publicly. Conversations about homosexual practice and attractions are kept for the backroom—if they happen at all. Jesus warns us what will happen to Jezebel and her advocates: '*I will cast her on a bed of suffering, and I will make those who commit adultery with her suffer intensely, unless they repent of her ways. I will strike her children dead.*'

These words of Jesus are not directed to Christians who are occasionally tempted by adultery, fornication or homosexual practice. All Christians experience sexual temptation at times. Rather, the judgment that Jesus pronounces is against those who unrepentantly teach and practice it. As for those of us who repent of sexual immorality instead of excusing or affirming it, we are told to '*hold on*'. The ride will be rough if we refuse to tolerate Jezebellic teaching and its advocates—but we expect seasons of opposition. Jezebels have danced in and out of history. They glory for a season, but Christ promises victory to his Bride. The question is, *will we join them, tolerate them, or stand firm against them when they come?*

Suicide Church

'I have this against you: you tolerate Jezebel.' -Rev 2

In the book of Revelation, the resurrected Jesus proclaims encouragement to his church in Thyatira, '*I know your deeds, your love and faith, your service and perseverance, and that you are now doing more than you did at first.*' Wouldn't you love to receive this commendation from Jesus? '*You're feeding and clothing the poor! You're socially active. You have a huge army of volunteers sacrificing their time for the good of others in the community. You have your own worship album. Well done!*' Who wouldn't be happy to hear this? Yet, Jesus then gives them a firm rebuke, '*Nevertheless, I have this against you: you tolerate that woman Jezebel, who calls herself a prophetess. By her teaching she misleads my servants into sexual immorality.*'

Jesus is addressing an insidious, ideological trend that's oozing straight out of Beelzebub's bumhole.

Appropriately, he uses the name 'Jezebel' to describe this 1st Century teacher and the fruit of her teaching. Jesus is saying that it gives his people a fake permission to be sexually immoral. It is sexual sin wrapped up in positive, educated, and religious language. The word that Jesus uses—the one we translate into 'sexual immorality'—is the Greek word *porneuō* (from which we get the modern word, pornography). It is a broad word that includes lots of specific, sexual sins: fornication, adultery, homosexual practice, incest, bestiality, etc.

Jesus' words are relevant to us in the UK and the USA. Why? Let's remember: Elijah never spoke to Jezebel—he rebuked Ahab for empowering her. John never spoke to Herodias—he rebuked Herod for marrying her. And here, Jesus is not rebuking this neo-Jezebel and her teaching. He is rebuking us: the Ahabs. He is rebuking us, his church, for tolerating this teaching of fake spirituality and fake sexuality. Apparently, there is a type of tolerance that Jesus hates. This is a hard truth for our current culture that has been nursed on a milky understanding of inclusivity since birth.

The problem with Jezebel is not just that she is in the world persecuting the church from the outside. We would expect that. But Jezebel is always

191

particular Elijahian ring about it as he calls for righteousness in the church and condemns spiritual adultery. He must have taken Elijah as an example for it is said of James that he had camel's knees. He spent so many hours each day on the hard floor wrestling back the powers of darkness, that it affected the shape of his legs. Legs like that might not make a woman into a fashion model, but they will be absolutely glorious to behold when we step into the other side of eternity.

James is not alone in church history. One great life to read about is that of Edward Payson or 'Praying Payson of Portland' as he has been called by some. He saw revival in the Congregational church he pastored in America. When he died and his body was removed from his bedroom, they found grooves worn into the hardwood floor next to his bed where he seesawed in constant prayer. Likewise, when they were preparing his body for burial, they found great camel pads on his knees—like James. The fruit of his ministry is still felt 200 years later in that region.

The greatest enemy to the church in 21st Century West is not Feminism, Nationalism, LGBTism, Racism, Atheism, or Mohammedism. Our chief sin, that makes us vulnerable in every other area, is our laziness after God. When the church rediscovers the power of God in faithfulness to Him in prayer and in his word, every poisonous ideology will be driven away like greasy smoke from cheap BBQ.

James, Elijah, and Praying Payson are not held up as spiritual superheroes so that we can feel condemned. Rather they help stretch our imaginations to what is possible this side of eternity. There is no limit that God sets on us in regards to divine closeness. None of us are guilty of asking Him for too much in regards to the coming of His Kingdom on Earth. We have Biblical and historical examples of how fallen men were not only saved by grace, but also empowered by the divine grace that they found in the prayer closet to change the world in their generations.

Entering the Closet

'He prayed.' -Jm 5

Prayer is the unwanted ginger-haired stepchild of the 21st Century Christian life. It is not very sexy. On the outside, it seems rather dull. *One just sits there… and talks to the sky?* Perhaps this is why UK and American Christians spend 50 minutes *a day* on social media and only 30 minutes *a week* in prayer. Our minds—raised in a generation that venerates social activism—struggles to understand what benefit investing hours in being alone in a prayer closet can possibly bestow upon the world. In an age when everyone is praised for coming out of the closet, why are we determined to shut ourselves in one?

Elijah knew why. He knew that the closet door concealed the nuclear reactor of the Christian life. It is where the power for all holy protesting comes from—be it a protest against our own personal sin or that of the world in which we live.

How does one begin to sum up the life and legacy of a man with as colossal a spiritual status as Elijah? James does it rather well in his epistle. Two words: *he prayed.* Prayer is the poetry the holy presence. The golden threshold of the prayer closet door frames for us a world of greater glory than any monarch's dream. Being children redeemed by the blood of Christ, we can now call God 'Abba' and share in his divine nature—an invitation to intimacy that even angels who muse in the moonlight will never fully grasp.

Meeting God in prayer changes us. It gives us strength in his love. But prayer not only changes us inwardly. It changes the world outwardly. Elijah's prayers did not merely craft his character into something more patient and kind. Prayer is more than just a Christianised form of meditation or self-control. Yes, there are times of peaceful prayer when our Father gently calms us and lifts fears. But we are also called to thunderous moments of world-changing intercession. Elijah's praying shut up the heavens for three years. Then they tore those same skies back open again. They scintillated a soaked sacrifice with a sea of searing flames. They called down napalmed judgement on unrepentant pagan soldiers.

We understand James to be the half-brother of Jesus. His epistle has a

Secondly, we not only need to have confidence that judgement will eventually come, but that God is in the act of saving people who are instruments of this wickedness while we wait. This is worth exercising patience for, because it may just be one of the greatest miracles one may witness in this age. We believe Jesus turned water into wine. But that pales in comparison to his ability to take a greedy, perverse man or woman and alchemise them into a godly, joyful soul—one that burns with holy fire.

When we speak to people who are tools of (dare we say it?) '*the Jezebel Spirit*', we need to embrace a tension. We are willing to rock the boat by firmly calling people to repentance. But we call them to turn, not because God does not love them, but because He does. It is unloving not to call Jezebel to repentance. She is not beyond Christ's power to redeem.

When we speak, we need discernment about the appropriate tone. There is a world of difference between how we speak to a young Christian who is sharing about their same-sex attraction for the first time and how we address an unrepentant teacher of immorality. Our words with the first will be marked by tenderness and compassion. Our words with the second will also be loving, but marked by firmness and the fire of truth.

And we must extend no welcome to fake teachers. We keep them out of our church if we can. To invite them in is not loving. It is an act of spiritual suicide. Inviting wolves into a place of influence in the name of love is an act of hatred to the flock. It is not even loving to the Jeze-wolf. It only confirms to them that their deeds and teaching are acceptable and can be tolerated when repentance is their chief necessity.

Every man or woman that we meet who is filled with Jezebellic attitudes, is a potential trophy for the grace of God. We extend to them truth in love while we hate their blasphemies. When the church has an Elijah sized heart for these slaves of Baal, we will pray rivers of compassionate tears and preach flames of holy words.

Grace for Jezebel

'I gave her time to repent.' -Rev 2

What is God's heart for Jezebel?

We like simple answers, but the answer to this is nuanced. And sometimes embracing nuance is key to our own spiritual maturity.

God hates the works of Jezebel. He hates her deeds, because he loves his church and this fake priestess and her teaching is a malignancy that could kill that church. God judges Jezebel by having eunuchs throw her off a tower and canines chow down her body. Jesus also throws the fake teacher that he labels as Jezebel onto a bed of suffering in the letter to the church Thyatira and he has her disciples die of the plague. With perfect hatred Jesus will punish her with violent judgements.

But not right away.

Scripture says that God *'has compassion on all that he has made'* (Ps 145). This includes fake teachers who corrupt His Bride. Ezekiel repeatedly says that God has no pleasure in the death of wicked people—but rather that they would repent and live (ch. 18 & 33). He will smite sinners—let no one tell you that God is no longer in the smiting business—but that is not usually his first recourse. He gives people time to repent. He does not have to. He does not always. But in love, He usually exercises great patience with us all. He gives a lot of time—and more than we deserve. He gave the Canaanites at least 400 years to repent before exterminating them (Gen 15). When was the last time you were patient with someone mocking you for 400 years?

We need to grasp this for two reasons. The first reason is that when we see Jezebellic influence in the church, we may wonder why God does not destroy it straight away. We see fake teaching and compromised living and know it's an offence to a holy God. In these times, we do well to remember that God will indeed punish sin in his time—but that he is far more patient than us. He will turn Jezebel into dog poo. But He first gives her time to get clean.

in order to exist. In the case of Asherah, Jezebel was tapping into the hunger all humanity has for beauty and life. She sought to (mis)lead Israel by offering them a poisonous drink—the wine of her ritual immorality. But the chalice was fake—it could never ultimately satisfy. But the thirst was not fake.

Like the ancient Israelis, we are designed for beauty. But this impulse gets hijacked. We spoke about pornography earlier, but it is the most obvious example. We join in the unending deluge of human stupidity each time we persist in the perilous viewing of accomplished or amateur porn stars. After a while, the visual whoring becomes boring. We're more depressed and self-absorbed than before because what we drink is not beauty done God's way.

Israel was susceptible to Jezebel's influence, because they were cut off from the beauty of God. It had been nearly a century since the days when King David played his harp and led the people of God in worship beautified by holiness. When people do not have the real, they become vulnerable to the fake. A man dying of thirst will quickly drink up a glass of salty water. The goal of the Christian is not just to lead people away from the poisons of sin, but to the wells of happy salvation.

One reason that Asherah had no power over Elijah's heart, was because he was caught up every day of his life in the beauty of Yahweh. Holiness captivated his heart with excitement. No shrine prostitute could compare. Worldliness—a word that most British preachers no longer use with any real conviction—had no grip on his soul. Jezebel and her seductions were dull by comparison to his vision of God. Elijah and his followers had souls that could resist fake worship only because they had the authentic.

The way we lead God's people in holiness is by showing them where to find the beauty their souls truly long to delight in. Sin has become so natural that we may not even recognise it at first. Like a sickly man poisoned by eating only junk food, one may need to develop the taste, to regularly experience it. But when one begins to drink of living water, there's simply no other drink that will satisfy our spiritual palate. This is why we need more than just correct theological information. That information needs to come alive and be fuel for our souls to worship. The theological must become doxological. We may need correct understanding in order to worship well, but merely having correct information does not automatically make a worshipper make.

The Morning Star

'I will also give him the morning star.' -Rev 2

Jesus encourages those in the church at Thyatira who are standing against Jezebel's infiltration. He speaks to them and to us. He calls us to hold fast to what we have—that we should not sell the truth he gives us nor yield in our stand for righteousness. He says that those who stand firm and obey until the end will receive authority over the nations. Those who stand against the seductive queen will rule as sanctified Kings. But Jesus does not end there—as if that promise was not enough to stretch even the liveliest of imaginations. He then says, almost like it was a bolt on item, *'I will also give him the Morning Star.'*

Does that promise seem a bit understated to you?

The Morning Star? Like, Venus? Sounds pretty yuuuge. But what does it mean? It was not just a nice sounding idea with no reality. Jesus is telling us a powerful truth about ourselves and how to overcome in this spiritual war.

There is a reason Jesus promised this particular reward to the church that was facing an onslaught from this vicar-vixen and her crew. Jezebel's goddess was Asherah—and the beautiful morning star was the symbol that represented this Canaanite deity. Jezebel led Israel in worship to her. If people wanted to get pregnant or spice up their sex life, they worshipped this yellow flame of the night sky under Jezebel's direction. People coveted this goddess—she was seen as life-giving beauty itself.

People rightfully desire beauty. Art, in its various forms, is an example. Be it a song, poem, or painting, art can contain a beauty so powerful that it changes or sustains us. It moves us to do, to speak, or to become something other than what we currently are. It inspires us to live. When Adam first sees the partner God prepared for him, it causes him to break out in poetic song (a seemingly popular occurrence for men that has survived both the fall and the millennia). He names this woman 'Eve' meaning *life*.

Though idolatry and fake worship are evil, they tap into a legitimate hunger inside of mankind. Evil is a parasite—it must pervert what is good

Apocalyptic Elijah

'I will give power to my witnesses and they will prophesy.' -Rev 11

There is much in the final book of the Bible I do not understand. Yes, I have read and studied it. But the more I read, the more my mind changes on what various metaphors might point to. But there is one thing I am confident of: Revelation is a tremendous book for adoration. The images it gives of the throne of God and the victory of the Lamb over the beast inspires all the children of God to worship. It is a book that enriches the heart even if it puzzles the mind at times. It is a book where poets have an easier time than systematic commentators. For that reason, when we look at the role Elijah plays in this culmination of redemptive history, we must do so humbly. We are looking at a passage where far greater minds than ours have acknowledged uncertainty.

Most commentators have historically agreed that the two witnesses in chapter eleven are Moses and Elijah. They are described using imagery from Zechariah chapter 4—they burn with God's fire as they draw oil from the olive tree of His word. They speak words of fire to a rebellious world who mock them and they are faithful witnesses even unto the point of death at the hands of the Beast.

We see that the Beast conquers the two preachers. He kills them and the world gets its clubbing clothes and gets sloshed in celebration. That which is rebellious against God is thrilled at the silencing of the church. Over 300 churches a year close in the UK, and many mockers think it is none too soon. In times and places where the church is persecuted more violently, there are parties on the streets as guns sing into the air when those from among their own clan are executed for embracing the gospel in 'honour killings'. In the 1950s in China, the Maoist revolutionaries happily threw out all missionaries to squash the small, Christian presence in the nation. The Beast is always at war against the bold witness of the Gospel.

But the church has a stubborn way of not staying dead. It falls into the ground, dies, but then shoots back up again. You know, empty tombs and

What is this Morning Star that Jesus gives to those who resist Jezebel? It is the holiness of Christ himself. In the closing words of Revelation, we read, *'I am the root and offspring of David, the bright and Morning Star.'* It is him. What Israel was really longing for when they went to worship Asherah was ultimately Christ. Only he could fulfil the longings for beauty and life that drove people to those shrines. Likewise, only Christ can fulfil the souls of those who give themselves over to sexual immorality in our day. In delighting in the holy worship of Christ, we have a light burning brightly within us that will sustain us in even the most apostate of generations.

Elijah's importunate, fiery praying and God's promise brought the rain. Prayer carries the promise to its gracious fulfilment. It takes persistent and persevering prayer to give the promise its largest and most gracious results.

-EM Bounds

stuff. When the church seems dead, '*the breath of God came into them, they stood on their feet and fear gripped those who saw them.*' So it has been throughout history. The Bible is the most attacked book in history, yet it is the best seller year after year. In China when Mao's revolution was over, the church had multiplied itself many times over and there are currently more Evangelicals there than in any country in Europe.

In Zechariah 4 we also read, '*Not by might, nor by strength, but by my Spirit says the Lord.*' In the last few decades, we have spent millions to try and reach Britain with the Gospel. But in spite of all our best efforts and marketing, we are worse off spiritually, morally, in overall attendance, in the growth of false religion, in the growing persecution of Christians, and in most measurable ways*. Many have been labouring hard, but it can feel discouraging when we get a broad view of things—because it seems the Beast is defeating us.

But he cannot. Not ultimately. We have the Breath of God. And this is why we're going to win. It won't be because we suddenly get multimillion pound budgets nor because a Christian gets to 10 Downing St or the White House. We've had all that and it has done next to nothing. We are going to win because a nameless, faceless army of people like you get sick of sin and compromise in the church and the world. They lock themselves in their room to pray until they are clothed with the breath of God to give and share with those God puts within their reach. No man and no method will get the glory. Yes, there will be identifiable leaders, but the move of God we pray for will be greater than anything we can attribute to a single person. God has repeatedly provided His church with the power they need when things look darkest. And it is that power that we must and shall receive from the Throne to be an Elijahian witness to our world again.

✒

---

* There are a few encouraging signs that buck the overall trend. Pentecostalism has been a growing movement with many real conversions. Teen Challenge has done great work reaching drug addicts. The percentage of Evangelicals within the CoE has grown. But the overall change in Christian profession and social morality has been a negative one in the UK.

mourn with those who mourn. And though we party with the angels when one sinner repents, we also weep when a denomination hardens its heart and walks away from God. In heaven, all tears will be wiped away. But in this life, holy men will know seasons of sorrow.

If the church is to fulfil its prophetic mission, there must be a place in our Christian discipleship for sackcloth and fasting. Throughout the Bible, fasting was an activity that people undertook to humble their bodies and souls in order to mourn when news of tragedy or judgement came. It was understood that, at the hearing of bad news, it was often appropriate to put a meal to the side and go be with God to weep.

On a merely natural level, Westerners have grief issues. We do not mourn thoroughly at times of disaster and often find ourselves much later having to psychologically process our losses—sometimes with the help of a therapist. Other cultures have better recognised that time and space needs to be given for a soul to process bad news—and that fasting helps us do this.

If we are to spiritually grow to the place where we can be entrusted with a message of repentance, we must have a sensitivity to that which grieves God's heart. Yes, we must also learn to gratefully celebrate his goodness. But there will also be times when we mourn and fast—not only our personal tragedies—but that which is tragic to the name and glory of God throughout the earth. We will not see the fruit of Elijah's boldness, if we do not know the fellowship of his tears.

Clothed in Sackcloth

'They will prophesy for 1,260 days clothed in sackcloth.' -Rev 11

Last week, a major denomination here in the UK announced that they would begin to recognise homosexual relationships as sacred marriage. Although this would have been seen as an unthinkable act for 99% of church history, this announcement passed with relatively little comment from church leaders of other denominations. There was no blowing of trumpet horns, no ashes, and no beating of the chests. There were no tears. Other denominations and churches did not assemble to mourn as Israel did in Judges 21 crying out *'Why, God, has Israel lost one of its tribes?'* Such compromise has happened before and we assume that it will happen again.

The apocalyptic witness of Moses and Elijah in Revelation 11—whether we see their appearance as something past, present, future, or some combination—gives us a glimpse into the prophetic call of the church in several ways. One of these is the description of their clothing: sackcloth.

This is not surprising given the descriptions of Elijah and John during their times of earthly ministry. Elijah and John both wore garments of camel's hair. Biblical commentator Joseph Benson writes of John's appearance out of the desert, *'Not, as some have supposed, a camel's skin, raw and undressed, but a kind of sackcloth, coarse and rough, made of the raw long hair of camels, and not of their fine and soft hair, dressed and spun into thread.'* Whatever else scholars may conclude about the significance of camel's hair clothing—we can know they were not party clothes.

There has never been much swag in sackcloth. The man who wears sackcloth is in protest—either in repentance at the sin of his own soul or in prayerful mourning over the sin of his people. A sackcloth heart is one that protests the status quo.

Christians are called to joy. We are called to laughter and to celebrate God's goodness and the blessings he delivers to us. Churches should be the happiest places on earth. And yet, we are not only to be happy. We are to have compassion. And sometimes compassion weeps. We are called to

Empire. Some Protestant Reformers perceived fake Elijah to be in the Roman Catholic Papacy. Others thought him to be Karl Marx and his socialism. Some see him as a yet to come, future figure.

Now there may be some truth to all of these. For now, let us simply understand this faux prophet as a spirit that incorporates yet transcends all of these manifestations. If what is written here seems a bit more abstract than other readings, please read slowly and up your caffeine intake.

One of the features of this spirit—whenever it manifests—is fake moralism or justice. There is an appeal to moral principles to try and get its own agenda across. Fake Elijah is reminiscent of Jezebel in this regard. She cried out that Elijah should be killed because he executed Baal's preachers. It was an effort to appeal to the '*eye for an eye, life for a life*' principle. In regards to Naboth's vineyard, she told the King that it was wrong for him to act the way he was acting and then had circumstances spun in order to make a righteous man look guilty. Those who persecute the church always disguise their hatred with some culturally acceptable, moral goal. They use an ethical mask in order to justify their malicious acts against the saints.

It may surprise some of you to hear that evil can be moral—but pagans can be Pharisees too. In the last few years in the West, we've seen the rise of food Pharisees as people adhere to particular diets with righteous zeal and label other people's food as 'bad'. But veganism imparts no virtue and one can be paleo and still be a pervert. Souls that are soured with sin still want to feel saintly, so they go on compensatory crusades over the food we eat, where we buy our clothes, what political party we MUST vote for, and other issues that help one feel righteous. All this activity allows them to look down on other people and feel less bad about their own guilt. Men who yell at their children and look at porn feel better about themselves because they drive an energy efficient car and campaign for wealth distribution. Their sense of personal accountability is lessened when they can blame some other social, political, or culinary group that they are not a part of as the main source of evil in this world. Many of today's social justice and moral crusades are driven by nothing less than a Satanic spirit.

And here a word about what is sometimes called 'national' or systemic' repentance is in order. There are indeed times when such repentance should be done. There are a few instances of this in the Scriptures. When all the facts are clearly established—and not just someone claiming to be in the know

Fake Elijah

'The second beast was like a lamb—it had two horns. But it spoke like a dragon!' -Rev 13

Will the real Elijah please stand up? Apparently, this question is—and will be—a thing. The book of Revelation is a poet's paradise with dramatic dichotomies around every canonical corner. There is a Christ on a white charger, and an anti-Christ who is a dragon. There is a joyful bride, and a drunken whore. There is a city that pollutes the Earth with sin, and a holy city coming down from God out of heaven.

There is also Elijah and fake Elijah. In chapter 11 we see Elijah with Moses. Then in chapter 13 we see the dragon's two champions. One is a beast out of the water and the other a beast out of the earth. The first beast can be seen as an anti-Moses. Just as Moses' name means *'drawn out of the waters'*, so this beast emerges out of the waters. Just as God revealed his name 'Yahweh' to Moses to give to Israel, so this beast will be covered in blasphemous names to proclaim to the earth.

The second beast is also easily compared and contrasted with Elijah and his ministry. Just like the real Elijah, the fake one also can call down fire from heaven. Both do powerful miracles. Just as the real Elijah restored the spirit of a dead boy, so the fake Elijah will impart a spirit to an image to make it (seemingly) come alive. Both affect the economy of nations. And it is here we need to pause and recognise just how much discernment we actually need if we seek to be sons of the prophets and disciples of Christ. There is a counterfeit Elijah movement at work in our world. There will be young adults who zealously give themselves to causes in the name of righteousness and justice, but they will be counterfeit. These movements will not be based on the Cross of Christ. They will be based on a humanistic impulse—hence they are marked with 666, the number of humanity.

As with many of the images in Revelations, commentators who are my intellectual superiors have a divergence of views on how this may have appeared in history. In early encounters, many Christians thought that Islam was the anti-Christ and Mohammed the fake prophet. Some have thought this beast to be a reference to the pagan priests in the Roman

And its power is in its appearance. This beast is the ultimate spin master. It postures with appeals of a quasi-Christian morality. But make no mistake—this dragon is a monster who will devour its opponent. The dragon is an evil that appeals for tolerance until it is in power—then it rains down punishment on the righteous. What it is really after has little to do with what it says it is after. Regardless of what it says, this dragon is not interested in equality. It is after power. The compassion language of 'siding with the oppressed' is little more than a cloak to cover its maddening rage against God and all that is truly righteous.

It was not long ago that the West was inhaling a prodigality of postmodern fumes. Upon hearing a Christian witness, people often retorted with, *'That may be true for you, but it's not true for me'* or *'Christianity may work for you, but I have my own truth. To each their own.'* But a society can only take this type of faux tolerance for so long before totalitarianism takes over. In urban Britain just try saying to two 'married' men, *'Gay marriage may be true for you but it's not for me.'* Or try refusing to use feminine pronouns for a man who thinks he is a girl. *'Yes, use whatever language you like for yourself, but that gender 'change' is just not true for me.'* You will then find that the trendiness of personalised truth has somewhat lessened of late.

This is the beast out of the Earth. Fake Elijah is the bully who portrays itself as the perpetual victim—a master of emotive words. In the name of justice, the dragon-lamb establishes totalitarianism.

because he saw a documentary online—then large-scale group repentance can be done.

But we live in an age where these things must be approached cautiously. Our generation has been trained to live guilt free, so we have the tendency to unload our guilty angst onto the nearest abstraction: the State, Big Business, Immigrants, Cis-White-Males, the Free Market, Labour, the Tories, Republicans, etc. The laws of the Universe cry out that sin must be punished. In order to satisfy this cry, we unload our psychological guilt onto 'the system'. We then whip it so that we can feel justice has been served and still walk away with unrepentant hearts of stone.

There *are* times when systemic repentance can and should happen. But the vast majority of moral instruction in Scripture, especially in the New Testament, is not given to 'the system'. It's given to the individual.

Fake Elijah has the ability to hijack people's moral compass in order to condemn that which is righteous and celebrate what is shameful. Whereas Elijah leads people in a movement of true righteousness and justice, fake Elijah leads a counterfeit justice movement not based on godly righteousness. This spirit manifests itself in the BDS movement against Israel or the Pro-Choice movement against unborn children. These movements promote wicked acts by hijacking moral language—often trying to disguise their work as one of liberation from oppression.

Just as Elijah called down the true fire of judgement, fake Elijah has its own fire. But this flame is man centred—it does not cause people to fall down in worship before a holy God.

Perhaps you have seen this happen to people around you in a subtle way. They begin their spiritual lives burning with a flame of contagious loyalty and affection for Jesus. But then they get swept up in a social or political cause. At first it all seems well-intentioned. After all, it aims to help people—something we should all want to do. But after a while your friend is no longer aglow for their Saviour. They are no longer humming hymns or praise songs. Instead they seem jaded and angry at those who are not joining their crusade. They have lots of zeal for changing this world—which in its proper perspective is not wrong. But they no longer have a vision for preparing people for the Eternity to come. Their method of changing the world does not centre on people bowing their knees to the true King. Their devotion to Christ has been distracted by this ancient serpent who appears like a lamb.

The first angel announces the *'eternal gospel'*. It calls the world to fear God and worship its creator. This is important to grasp. Many of us preachers are so enamoured with the heart of the gospel—what Christ has done for us through his cross and resurrection—that we forget the response to his work which is also part of the gospel. We are to persuade men as well as to instruct them. Jesus said that this gospel is one of *'repentance and forgiveness of sins'* (Lk 24). As Peter pleaded with the crowds at the birth of the church *'save yourselves from this wicked generation!'* If the call to worship and fear God is not part of our gospel witness, then we have left something essential out.

These men have the opposite mission to that of the beasts and their minions. Their message of repentance clears the air created by the beasts' blasphemous bulletins that they issue to all the world. Repentance calls on mankind to take responsibility for evil. Blasphemy accuses God of that evil. Unrepentant men must blasphemy because they must deal with sin. It is a reality we can't escape from. If we won't take responsibility, confess, and fall on God's mercy, then blasphemy will be our final end. These men stand as God's apologists and show the world that it is not God who has brought evil to the world, it is they who have done so.

The second and third angels give us the confidence to stand in the face of both temptation and persecution. The second angel announces the end of Babylon the Great—that great systemic Jezebel. She will not seduce and mislead the simple and naïve forever. She will not always be able to ensnare God's children with her kisses and her lies.

The third angel announces the end of the Fake Moses and Elijah and the judgement of those who receive the blasphemous mark. It may initially seem that those who refuse the mark of our godless age are losing out. It may seem that they're *'on the wrong side of history'* as so many have said. But in the end, all they have missed out on is the wrath of God. We can rest assured of victory. Whereas Elijah is taken up to God in a chariot of fire, Fake Elijah is thrown by God into a lake of fire. Those who have accused God of moral guilt, find that it is they who are guilty. The secrets of all hearts will be revealed and men will no longer be able to hide behind the mountainous layers of lies that they spent their whole lives telling themselves.

These 144,000 are Christocentric in devotion, righteous in character, and fearless in proclamation. They are slandered and misrepresented, yet they remain steadfast. Do we want to be among their number? The spiritual

144,000 Men & Apocalyptic Angels

'They had His name written on their foreheads.' -Rev 14

We are called to holy war against the dragon. It's no accident that the description of those following the dragon's two beasts is immediately followed by a description of those who follow the Lamb. I confess an uncertainty over what the cryptic number 144,000 may refer to—though I've read several opinions. But it is significant that, unlike those with 666 written on their foreheads, these men have the name of Christ and their heavenly Father tattooed on theirs. That is clear enough to understand. Those who follow the fake Elijah have their first loyalty to humanity. Those who are sons of the prophets are loyal to God's lamb—and follow him where he goes. They have the first and second greatest commandments in proper order.

We have already discussed the sons of the prophets in the days of Elijah and Elisha. In his vision, John sees these Elijah Men animated in apocalyptic fashion. They are honest—they do not lie or manipulate things with half-truths. They keep their word to people even when it hurts. They also have not *'defiled themselves with women'* and they sing the praises of God. Apparently, there are some songs that only holy men can sing. This is why in days of fierce spiritual battle, men must guard their hearts and their pants alike. We must rid ourselves of idols and sexual immorality and all of Jezebel's tricks if we are to be men who have strength to resist fake Elijah. We are to praise the Lamb with boldness. And brother, when we taste the freedom that comes from Christ's redemption, we will sing a song for the whole world to hear. These songs give God's men courage and strength to stand in the face of the fire rained down upon them from the Beasts. As Martin Luther wrote in his famous song, *'The Prince of Darkness grim, we tremble not for him; his rage we can endure, for lo his doom is sure. One little word shall fell him.'*

But the sons of the prophets do not walk alone. They have angels. Three angels fly with them and work with them in proclaiming these three great truths that Elijah and John echoed throughout their earthly ministries and that God's men need to daily breath and share with the world.

The waters where the woman was seated are peoples, nations and languages.

-Rev 17.15

Rejoice over her heaven, saints, and prophets: God has judged her for you.

-Rev 18.20

#ElijahMen

leadership of Israel was not a responsibility Elijah was born with. Ahab should have been a leader of Yahweh worship. But he dropped that responsibility. Elijah picked it off of the ground and ran with it though he did not have to. He grew shoulders in prayer that became broad enough to carry a mantel that was greater than his obligation. He decided to grow strong because he saw that other men were weak.

He was not Israel's King by birth. He was not a priest. He was not an ordained man. But he became God's man. And God's men take responsibility for spiritual messes that are not their fault.

These sons of prophets repent of their people's sins though they are not the ones personally committing them. They are not content to live in their own little bubble of spirituality. They are not satisfied with merely reading books or participating in contemplative retreats while their world skips down the pretty slopes to hell. They don't just pray for their own peace of mind—they get on their knees and raise their hands to battle hell and change the destinies of others. They refuse to accept the status quo as long as their churches exist comfortably compromised with prayerless families and fake teaching. Because they ache for the sin of their people, they cannot be quiet—not before God and not before man. They pray, and they preach. They weep, and they write. They cry, and they converse. The weight of our sad times invites us to receive and give riots of grace.

How wretched would it be of us to let things merely be?

Do you think that the devil is going to allow you to have a life of burning holiness and disciplined prayer without a struggle? Do you think that the fake teachers who have brought blasphemy into the church are going to give up without a fight? Do you think they'll just hand you your church back without it costing you scars? If you want your soul and church back, you will have to fight every single day of your life.

But you are a son of God. You are one of the chosen. A sanctified scallywag. You have been reborn to a life of battle. Let the Beast, let Jezebel, let heresy, let your own flesh come with all the fury hell can muster. Yes, the war will bring its wounds. But God can redeem those scars and turn them to glory. His grace is more than sufficient. Both the fairy tales and Christian theology agree: dragons exist for us to defeat.

Scriptures and the power of the Spirit towards almost any socio-political cause. She infiltrates souls and congregations alike. She is Fake Church.

But have courage. John's revelation displays the scene of her destruction. Just as King Jehu judged Jezebel from his war chariot, so our greater King Jesus '*judges the great prostitute*' from his battle horse. As dogs ate Jezebel's body, so two beasts now '*devour her flesh*'. The feminine form once coveted by Kings is chewed by the cruellest of critters. She is judged—and the power of her allure shatters like stemware on stone.

In eternity, our souls are no longer soured by sin. Our inner Ahabs are buried and we are free. We love with liberated embrace, untainted by shadows of impropriety, jealousy, or fear of unrequited affection. We arrive at a sea of true and perfect love. The counterfeit is gone.

The blood that spilt from our bodies in heralding the gospel did not fall silently into earth's soil. The Universe's Judge has heard the cry of every innocent drop. Our own hands renounced vengeance because we knew our Avenger would be faithful. We knew because we read the culmination of the Holy Book where time ends and eternity begins.

Now, the New Jerusalem arrives. The voice of the Bridegroom shouts in celebration. God's people party, for there is no more perversion to protest. Our protesting is done; paradise is here. Once persecuted saints now laugh as they feast on meat, not brought by ravens, but by angels. Battle-scarred prophets raise their glasses in cheer. There is now and forever only a glorious Bride. And the only thing left of the ancient sorceress, who lifted herself to heights of worldly glory, are the turds of banished and burning beasts.

The Whore is nevermore.

Jezebel: The Final Defeat

'When I saw the woman, I was amazed.' -Rev 17

Babylon. Special attention is given this femme fatale in the final pages of Scripture. John sees her and his mouth drops open in amazement. He has already introduced us to one Jezebel at the beginning of his vision. She was a local fake teacher. Now he uses similar language to describe a global city personified as a woman wrapped in colourful clothes that bewitches the whole world and tries to corrupt the people of God with sexual immorality and idolatry. Her beauty is a terror. This Jezebel does not desire to merely manipulate one King. This grander Jezebel makes all the Earth's rulers and mighty men *'drunk on the wine of her sexual immorality'*. She militarises her magnetism. All the seduced gather round. They drool over her breasts and legs, are mesmerised by her dark eyes, and hunger to be lost in her hills and valleys. Like a magnificent black hole, she consumes whatever comes near.

There are two ways to understand this monstrous mistress. One way to view her is as the part of our world that delights in revolution against God. She is the cities of the earth that define themselves by sexual immorality and sophisticated idolatry. She is the dark side of Sodom, Corinth, Ancient Rome, 1930s Berlin, San Francisco, Vegas, Bangkok, Rio, and Amsterdam. She is the sites you visit online before you erase your browsing history. She has manifested herself in big ways throughout history, and will continue in even grander displays before the End. She is the counterpart to the Beast who influences through force and authority. She prefers to pull people into darkness with charm—not threats.

We may also see her as the phantom that allures God's people in every age to compromise. The Beast persecutes Christ's Bride from the outside. Jezebel corrupts her from within. Yes, the queen can be terribly totalitarian once fully enthroned. But she gets there craftily—one innocent compromise at a time. Though hell delights to see the holy Bride beaten down, it prefers to see her sell out. That's why Jezebel pulls us away from the wholehearted worship of Yahweh and his Christ. She takes us from loyalty to the

Goodbye

(What do we do now?)

That was Elijah's story. At least as far as the canon goes. But church history is still being written, and we need those who walk in the spirit of Elijah as much as Israel ever did.

Thank you for taking time to read this book. If you wish to share bits of this book through social media or stories about how God is stirring revival in your area, please use the hashtag #ElijahMen and let's see if we can network together those with ravenous hearts for the things of God. It has been the prayer of the writer and his praying friends that it will both ignite and strengthen the flames of holiness inside of you. For further reading, I recommend the 19th Century EM Bound's book, *Power in Prayer*.

Last century, Leonard Ravenhill continually asked the church, *'Where are the Elijahs of God?'* It is with this question in mind that I leave you. The church in the UK (or whatever nation you may be in) needs you. This challenge is particularly for young men—but those of you who do not fit into that category may cerainly respond as you see fit before God. It is:

I will be a man who…

I. *Through grace reforms himself by repenting of sin daily and confessing when needed to trusted Christians. I will put to death my inner Ahab and feast upon the meat of God's prophetic word.*

II. *Prays and works for repentance, revival, and reformation in my church and nation.*

III. *Speaks God's truth with courage and compassion to a world filled with people who are both rebellious and broken.*

IV. *I will do the above things until my chariot comes.*

Grace to all of you who love Jesus.

Where is the God of Elijah? He's where he has always been: waiting for Elijah to call on him.

-Leonard Ravenhill

The Author

Joshua D. Jones tweets, reads, prays, and smokes pipe tobacco in his yellow armchair in Therfield, England. He enjoys his family and meeting up with his best friends for quality coffee, food, and conversations about everything and nothing. He gets to pastor Therfield Chapel—a delightful church full of fun and ferocious saints and frolics in fields of nouns, verbs, and alliterating adjectives over at his blog, Sanitys-Cove.com.

If the book has helped you spiritually man up, please let him know. He's happy to hear from scallywags for Jesus the world over and welcomes dialogue. Also, if you'd like to contact him about speaking or writing, he can be reached at:

Twitter: @BlueCheezWhisky
Email: ElijahMenEatMeat@Gmail.com
#ElijahMen